Self-Esteem for Women:

A Woman's Guide to Recognizing Self-Worth and Understanding and Fixing Low Self-Esteem

Margaret Douglas

AF256305

©Copyright 2021 – *Margaret Douglas* - All rights reserved

The content contained within this book may not be reproduced, duplicated, or transmitted without direct written permission from the author or the publisher.

Under no circumstances will any blame or legal responsibility be held against the publisher, or author, for any damages, reparation, or monetary loss due to the information contained within this book, either directly or indirectly.

Legal Notice

This book is copyright protected. This book is only for personal use. You cannot amend, distribute, sell, use, quote or paraphrase any part, or the content within this book, without the consent of the author-publisher.

Disclaimer Notice

Please note the information contained within this document is for educational and entertainment purposes only. All effort has been executed to present accurate, up to date, and reliable, complete information. No warranties of any kind are declared or implied. Readers acknowledge that the author is not engaging in the rendering of legal, financial, medical, or professional advice.

Table of Contents

Introduction

Self-esteem is a person's opinion of themselves which can range from "I am worthless" to "I am great". Self-esteem may be a product of one's life experiences, social companionship, group membership, or even the beliefs of a particular culture.

Self-esteem is different from self-acceptance; acceptance does not mean that one accepts being whatever he/she is and whatever makes one change their behavior. Self-acceptance is a way of life guided by the individual toward improving self-confidence. Self-esteem is about the evaluation of one's own worth based on self-perspective. Self-esteem may be determined by various factors: the result of a test, the assessment of peers, or evaluative judgments made by third parties.

It's a simple equation really. Your self-esteem equals the level of respect you have for yourself. If your level of respect is high, your self-esteem will be high, and vice versa. For this reason, there is no easy "fix" for gaining higher self-esteem or boosting it in someone else. The best approach is to work together to create an environment that honors the individual and supports their growth in confidence and happiness.

Self-esteem is a person's opinion of themselves. It may be positive or negative. If someone has low self-esteem, they might feel worthless or inferior. If someone has high self-esteem, they might feel confident and superior to others. The self-estimate of a person can vary from good to bad as per his environment and time period. Self-esteem is affected by judging oneself falsely or through the value they give to the people around them.

There are two types: objective and subjective. Objective self-esteem is the value a person places on himself or herself in relation to the outside world. Subjective self-esteem is the value the person places on himself or herself as a result of their own feelings about themselves. A person's subjective sense of self-esteem may be affected by cognitive distortions and or illusions.

Self-esteem is often described as being an inner, intuitive concept, but many psychologists have begun to measure it subjectively, rather than objectively. The use of subjective measures in psychology allows researchers to correlate human behavior with the perception and experience of the individual. In particular, self-esteem can be measured via the Rosenberg Self-Esteem Scale (RSE), which measures self-esteem by looking at answers to questions regarding how one feels about oneself.

Other methods for assessing self-esteem are psychological tests, exams like the ABZ (American Board of Examiners in Psychology), or subjective assessments by peers, family members, or therapists. Some tests and exams measure the capacity to reach a goal (e.g., intelligence test) as well as the skills required to solve problems (e.g., intelligence test) rather than with objective measures of numbers or quality. It is often believed that those with high self-esteem generally exhibit a healthy sense of confidence, while those with low self-esteem tend to have more unhealthy personality traits.

Self-esteem theory can be traced back to the 3rd century B.C. According to Aristotle, "the basis of optimism is self-confidence." He believed that individuals become courageous and are able to face danger when they believe themselves to be capable and competent. Aristotle was the first to examine the theory that people might assess themselves lower than their actual or true level.

The sociologist Charles Horton Cooley in 1902 presented his idea of the looking glass self (based on an 1892 paper by William James), which talks about how people look to others for approval and their own self-worth. His basic idea was that one forms one's identity based on how others view them. It was not until 1933, however, that a manual for mental health clinicians described a therapeutic technique based on the concept of learned helplessness from the theories of Seligman and Maier-Seligman, who contended that "learned helplessness" could be overcome by making patients aware that controllable events were actually controlled by them.

The term "self-esteem" was used by Norman Vincent Peale in 1952 to describe a positive mental attitude, and it subsequently was explored in more detail by Abraham Maslow in his 1954 paper "The concept of self-actualization." Maslow's paper became part of most psychology textbooks and helped generate a lot of interest in self-esteem as a psychological concept.

According to recent studies, it is now clear that both subjective and objective measures can be used to gauge people's levels of self-esteem. In one study, participants were shown a video about their soccer team, either before they had been given the RSE or after. There were significant differences between the scores after and before, showing that a person's self-esteem can be measured objectively.

Prior to the research done by Rosenberg, a study by Coopersmith found that people who consider themselves more physically attractive tend to have higher self-esteem than those who consider themselves less physically attractive. Another study conducted by Lewis Terman in 1954, a year before Rosenberg's scale, found that students' ratings on physical appearance correlated highly with their self-esteem scores on scales given by Coopersmith and Julian Rotter. In addition, self-esteem is widely considered a significant factor in an individual's attitude and behavior.

Numerous studies assert that self-esteem is an essential element in success. Despite the popularity of this claim, other researchers allege that factors such as personality, intelligence, and interpersonal abilities are more important than self-esteem in determining personal success.

A 2010 study published in "Psychological Bulletin" discovered that there is a strong relationship between high self-esteem and good mental health at the national but not at the personal level. Individuals with high self-esteem tend to have better mental health whether they live in wealthy nations or developing ones. They also tend to be more satisfied with their lives and feel more content with themselves.

Self-esteem is beneficial for health and it is not a gross overstatement to describe it as essential for mental health, if not constituting the core element of mental health itself. However, several important components are missing from the theoretical explanation, First, there is the lack of empirical evidence showing that self-esteem leads to improvement in mental health. Second, there is no explanation why self-esteem should be protective in settings where societal barriers appear to hinder success. Finally and most important, there is no evidence that self-esteem enhances subjective well-being.

The present meta-analysis aims to address these limitations. In particular, it seeks to determine whether high self-esteem is associated with good health in the general population. We further want to explore whether high self-esteem buffers the negative effects of societal factors and thus serves a protective function.

Research has focused on different parameters of self-esteem. Some empirical research suggests that high self-esteem is associated with lower mortality and higher marital success among adults; however, it is not correlated with improved job performance among adolescents or younger adults. Other researchers are cautious about linking self-esteem and physical health outcomes. One study indicates that there is no relationship between self-esteem and mortality.

One study suggests that children and adolescents with high self-esteem are more likely to engage in antisocial or aggressive behavior. Another study also found a significant relationship between high self-esteem and deviant behavior in children as well as adults. Specifically, children with high self-esteem were more likely to violate rules and to exhibit disruptive, aggressive, or destructive behavior. Adults with high self-esteem were more likely to violate traffic laws, engage in physical fights, use physical threats or intimidation in a bar setting, indulge in illegal drugs, and drink alcohol at a risky level.

Low self-esteem and anxiety are two of the most common mental health problems in the world. I'll talk about a few ways that you can start to build up your self-esteem and become more confident. Self-esteem is one of those traits that can dramatically affect every aspect of your life, from how much money you make to how happy you feel. As you would expect, it has an effect on our mental health.

Most of us feel pretty good about ourselves fairly often. In fact, I don't know a single person who is completely happy with everything about themselves. Even the most beautiful and rich person on earth has some things that they don't like about their life or themselves. It's just a part of being human.

Despite so much interest, there is no official measurement of self-esteem, but there are definitely signs to look out for. The main one is people acting like they are superior to everyone else around them. This could manifest a variety of ways and may not always be obvious at first. If someone talks down to wait staff or service professionals, they likely have a problem with their own self-esteem.

There is a lot to uncover and learn so read on.

Chapter 1
Understanding Self-Esteem

What is self-esteem?

Self-esteem refers to the image we have of ourselves regarding how much value we place on our lives. And developing self-esteem is about respecting ourselves, believing in our worth, and building the capacity to feel "good enough" just as we are. Self-esteem is not about gaining the approval of others around us or being perfect. It is about learning to accept yourself and preserving the belief that you are a great person simply because you are a human being.

Intrinsic self-worth can be a tricky concept to wrap your brain around. It may be something you've never really considered before; it might tap into personal and existential belief systems, or it may seem just plain foreign due to years of struggles with poor self-esteem. Rather than debate the basis or validity of internal worth, I invite you to step back from any doubt or block beliefs that prohibit you from accepting your sense of self-worth. Think about how you might view a new baby, a child, or a close friend. Chances are you would easily see their value, yet when self-esteem is low, it may be difficult to believe you possess that same level of fundamental worth.

When our self-esteem is low, we tend to measure ourselves with more severe standards than we do with the rest of the world. As you work through this book, challenge yourself to let go of any resistance and trust that you, too, have inherent worth. When you put aside your reservations, you will be better able to commit to utilizing the recommended steps and tools to build self-esteem. As your self-esteem begins to improve, you will find the veil that prevented you from believing in your worth has lifted.

You perhaps already have a good idea, but let's start at the beginning and ask what is self-esteem? Self-esteem is our assessment of ourselves. It is essentially a measure of self-worth and importance. When this self-assessment is positive, we consider ourselves valuable and useful and develop high self-esteem. When it is negative, we feel useless, incompetent, and unhappy, and our self-esteem remains low. Self-esteem is an essential part of the personality that has been forged in the early years. Self-esteem increases or weakens considerably, depending on your success or failure and your reaction to any critical situation in life.

Let's imagine that you set a goal for improving your self-esteem in a month. Realistically speaking, it is hard to achieve that kind of shift in attitude within one month. Once you set this goal and don't gain it, you will have to make do with whatever progress you make. If you're unable to reach the goal or achieve the objective you have in mind, you will further slip into the pit of depression and not achieve what you have in mind.

Why is Self-Esteem Vital to a Person?

Self-esteem is known as a person's beliefs about their value and worth. It also concerns the feelings people feel about their dignity or unworthiness. Self-esteem is important because it strongly influences people's choices and decisions. In other words, self-esteem plays a motivating role, making people more or less likely to take care of themselves and unravel their full potential.

People with high self-esteem are motivated to take care of themselves and constantly persevere to achieve their personal aspirations. People with low self-esteem do not tend to see themselves as worthy of happy outcomes or able to reach them and, therefore, they tend to slip on important things and become less persistent and resistant in overcoming adversity. They may have the same goals as people with higher self-esteem but are generally less motivated to pursue them to completion.

Self-esteem is a rather abstract concept that's hard for someone who doesn't yet have to understand. One way for people with low self-esteem to start appreciating what it would be like to have better self-esteem is to consider how they feel about the things in their life that they enjoy. For example, some people like cars. Since cars are important to them, these people take care of their cars. They make good decisions on where to park the car, how often to fix it, and how to drive it. They can decorate the car and show it to others with pride. Self-esteem is like that, except that you love and care about yourself. When children believe they are precious and important, they take care of themselves. They make good decisions that increase their value instead of breaking it.

Developing and maintaining healthy self-esteem is a process that can take time, yet it is such a worthwhile endeavor for us all. Imagine how much simpler life could if we simply loved and accepted ourselves. We all stand to benefit from building self-esteem in some way. Both men and women can utilize the recommended tools to boost self-esteem. However, they must overcome challenges and take charge of their lives with confidence and improved self-esteem.

There are many definitions of self-esteem and related concepts; however, the following definition is crafted especially for certain ages. I encourage you to keep it in mind as you work through the material in the book: healthy self-esteem is about holding a positive, realistic, and consistent image of yourself that demonstrates self-respect, a sense of unwavering self-worth, and an acceptance that you deserve happiness and fulfillment despite life's imperfections, stereotypes, challenges, and setbacks.

We have narrowed down and defined self-esteem and how it differs from similar constructs. Read on to find out what sets self-esteem apart from other self-managing characteristics and states.

Self-Concept vs. Self-Esteem

Self-esteem is different from one's self-concept, although self-esteem may be part of self-concept. Self-concept is our perception of ourselves, our responses when we ask the question, "Who am I?" It's about knowing our trends, thoughts, preferences and habits, hobbies, skills, and weaknesses. In other words, the consciousness of who we are is our concept of ourselves.

Self-Image vs. Self-Esteem

Another comparable term with a different meaning is self-image; self-image is similar to self-concept because it is the way you see yourself. Instead of being based on reality, it can be based on false and inaccurate thoughts. Our self-image may be close to or distant from reality, but it is generally not completely aligned with objective reality or the way others perceive us.

Self-Worth vs. Self-Esteem

Self-esteem is a concept similar to self-worth, but with a small difference (although important): self-esteem is what we believe,

think, and feel about ourselves, while self-worth is the most com-
prehensive recognition that we are precious human beings worthy of love.

Self-Confidence vs. Self-Esteem

Self-esteem is not self-confidence; self-confidence is about trusting yourself and your ability to take on challenges, solve problems, and get involved in the world successfully. As you have
probably noticed in this description, self-confidence is based
more on external measures of success and value than on internal
measures that contribute to self-esteem. You may have great self-
confidence, especially in a specific area or field, but you still lack
a healthy sense of worth or general self-esteem.

Self-Efficacy vs. Self-Esteem

Like self-confidence, self-efficacy is also linked to self-esteem, but
it is not an indirect indicator. Self-efficacy is known as the belief
in one's ability to perform certain tasks. You can be very effective
in playing basketball but have poor self-efficacy when it comes to
success in math lessons. Unlike self-esteem, self-efficacy is more
specific than global and is based on external success and not internal value.

Self-Compassion vs. Self-Esteem

Finally, self-esteem is not self-compassion. Self-compassion focuses on our relationships with ourselves, not how we judge ourselves or how we perceive ourselves; being compassionate means being kind and forgiving yourself and avoiding being harsh or overly critical of yourself. Self-compassion can lead to a healthy feeling of self-worth, but it is not, in itself, self-esteem.

Factors that Affect Self-Esteem

Self-esteem plays an important role in your life and has a profound impact on the choices you make. Self-esteem determines what you consider yourself capable and worthy of doing. When you have low self-esteem, you run a greater risk of not reaching your true potential. Many factors influence self-esteem by either increasing or decreasing your self-esteem.

Your Childhood

Your childhood is one of the main factors that contributes self-esteem. While growing up, as your personality and body grow, everyone you know can impact who you become – meaning your degree of self-esteem. For instance, kids who grow up in unstable families tend to have less self-confidence and self-esteem and often end up carrying this burden throughout their lives.

The Media

Our total obsession with the media, be it social media, television, or print advertising, contributes to society's vast self-esteem issues. Instant access to social media is particularly detrimental to young minds, with the constant pressure to appear and act as public models, celebrities, and peers. It is best controlled to say the least.

The Workplace

Most of our time is spent at school or work, depending on our age. The environment we engage in influences all aspects life, including self-esteem. If you are in a stressful and overly demanding job, you can count on some low self-esteem. Working in a productive and encouraging environment can positively influence your self-esteem so you become stronger. Many factors influence your self-esteem. Any part of your life can, but the person who has the most say over your self-esteem is you. Start giving yourself good messages about who you are, and stop fighting improving your self-esteem.

A Healthy Lifestyle

A healthy lifestyle is imperative to having positivity. You must make sure that your life is healthy. People usually feel better about themselves and get a boost of confidence, when the act of exercising discharges hormones that impart an ecstatic feeling. It will help you feel like you are doing something meaningful and joyful. Exercise is healthy, and it should be non-negotiable in your life.

Accepting Rejection

Positive thinkers can accept rejection. Much like with failure, they can acknowledge when things go wrong, and they usually can accept whatever has happened. If they apply for something and are denied it, they may be upset or disappointed, but they can accept it. They can fight or appeal the decision, but they accept that sometimes has failed even if they tried their best, and they do not let them lose track of what matters most.

Chapter 2
Self-Esteem: Learn to Respect Yourself

Respect Yourself

Knowing who you are and caring for yourself are fundamental steps in developing the necessary understanding and self-compassion needed to reclaim self-worth. However, you can't truly develop and maintain a healthy self-esteem until you can consistently respect yourself. While self-esteem involves how you think and feel, self-respect is about your actions. How you act and interact with others and the choices related to your level of self-respect ultimately play a role in your view of self-worth. Self-respect, along with a determination to begin making healthier choices, will help you make the most of the tools provided in this book.

Quashing the Need to Please

Looking over the list of values you selected as important to you, reflect upon this: how often do you pursue goals aligned with these values? And do you expect others to demonstrate these values in their interactions with you to the same extent you demonstrate them toward others? I know it's tricky, but one of the consequences of low self-esteem is that we often work hard to uphold these values in our interactions with others, sometimes sacrificing our wishes and needs. We deny ourselves the same level of respect in return. This tendency is caused by the approval-seeking characteristic of low self-esteem.

Think about how often you defer to others, perhaps allowing them to make choices and decisions for you. Over time, this can result in losing sight of your identity and straying from your path as you submit to becoming a follower. Do you ever agree to things you know you don't want to do or put aside your wishes and endeavors while going along with others?

Think about what drives this need to please. Where does your tendency to accommodate others or put their needs first come from? Reflect on your experiences, especially regarding gender roles, as you were growing up. Were there any messages conveyed about your role as a female?

As you work to break the pattern of people-pleasing, start paying attention to your own needs and make yourself more a priority. You can begin evening out the playing field in your relationships and interactions with others as you work to establish a greater level of self-respect.

While it is important to respect others, it's equally important to avoid constantly sacrificing your own needs to avoid conflicts or appease others. The goal is to create more equality in relationships and end the cycle of denying your rights and worth. As you move forward, pay attention to your self-talk and watch out for any distorted beliefs that force you to assume you are obligated to meet everyone else's needs at the expense of your own. You have the right to your happiness, safety, and emotional well-being.

Developing Assertiveness

After years of being a people-pleaser and sacrificing your own needs in favor of others, it can be difficult to make changes. As you learn to value your rights, needs, and the importance of making yourself a priority, it can help to equip yourself with some tools as you are essentially learning a new language—the language of saying "no, thank you!"

As always, continue monitoring your self-talk and working to change any distorted thinking that prevents you from speaking up or protecting yourself from the things you do not want to take on. Watch out for that destructive internal critic telling you that you are not worthy or deserving of respect. It simply is not true. Seeking to obtain mutual respect in relationships creates an equality that everyone benefits from.

Both men and women with people-pleasing tendencies and low self-esteem often act in passive ways, so learning and developing assertiveness tools is an important part of their journey. Contrary to what you may think, assertiveness is not an inborn trait or a characteristic of only naturally confident people. Rather, it's a skill that can be learned, practiced, and cultivated to help you navigate all kinds of situations and ultimately foster better self-respect.

Think about somebody you admire for her ability to be assertive. Assertiveness involves the ability to express your opinions, preferences, needs, limits, and boundaries in a respectful, polite way. Assertiveness is not like aggression, which includes force, threats, and hostility. Assertiveness is an art and a gift—it involves communication that is direct, honest, and firm, yet respectful and aimed at creating harmony in relationships, rather than engaging in power struggles or a need for control. Read on to learn more about it. It may be comforting to know that you can develop assertiveness.

Some strategies to hone your ability to act assertively include:

You reframe distorted thinking. When you reflect on situations, stop and look at what may have held you back from being assertive. Consider "what would have been a better response?"

Creating affirmations. These affirmations can be designed specifically to support assertiveness— "I am learning to speak my mind," "I can handle conflict with confidence and ease," and "I have the right to my thoughts and opinions."

Practice. Whether you choose to role-play with a friend or practice in front of the mirror, spend time acting out responses to different situations. Practice speaking with a confident voice and a calm body.

Avoiding High-Risk Behaviors

Without assertiveness skills and healthy outlets, both men and women with low self-esteem and issues of depression and anxiety sometimes turn to risky, self-destructive behaviors as a way to cope. Unhealthy coping strategies may include excessive drinking, drugs, promiscuity, or self-harmful behaviors. Initially, this can happen due to peer pressure or relinquishing your power to gain approval or feel wanted. While these activities may temporarily provide relief or distraction from the difficult emotions you are struggling with, they only serve as a Band-Aid over a greater problem that needs to be addressed.

Trying to build worth, gain approval, or decrease negative feelings by utilizing unhealthy coping mechanisms creates a vicious cycle, likely to leave you feeling even worse about yourself between fixes. Ultimately, these things are self-destructive and further damage self-esteem, in addition to creating serious and potentially dangerous health concerns and devastating problems with addiction.

If you are utilizing self-destructive behaviors as a way of coping, make a promise to stop immediately. If you are unable to stop these behaviors on your own, seek out the help of a qualified professional who can support you through the process.

Trusting Yourself

Part of respecting yourself involves developing self-trust. It can be challenging when self-esteem is low, especially after years of doubting your worth, but trust can be cultivated and developed like assertiveness. Learning to trust your gut, your ability to make appropriate decisions, and your feelings' validity are important pursuits as you develop faith in yourself and make changes to support a healthier future. Self-trust is an important component to following through with the steps in this program. Sometimes, having an objective and supportive third party to hold you accountable can help you work through the issues that threaten your progress.

Ways to begin the process of learning to trust yourself are:
1. speak kindly to yourself
2. avoid people who undermine your self-trust
3. keep promises to yourself

These three things align perfectly with the steps and goals we are discussing regarding building self-esteem. As you continue banishing the negative, distorted self-talk filled with preoccupation about what others think, replace these thoughts with self-talk that nurtures your gut instincts and abilities. Observe how you view situations in various experiences and focus on your body's emotions and physical sensations. They can serve as a guide to tuning in to your thoughts, beliefs, and personal requirements. Trust yourself to handle appropriately or walk away from uncomfortable situations.

As you work to develop self-respect and end the drive to people-please, avoid people who make this endeavor difficult for you. You may not have avoided these people in the past, but as you increase your awareness, you can choose to take control and make better choices about your relationships. We will talk more about ways to maintain healthy boundaries and supportive relationships.

You have already committed to reading this book and have made it this far—that is great news! Keep the momentum going by promising yourself to follow through with your journey to improve self-esteem! Meanwhile, continue practicing and ensuring you are utilizing the tools you've learned so far as you prepare to move on to the final two steps.

You learned that developing a kind, affirmative internal voice filled with positive messages is at the forefront of every attempt to better care for and respect yourself. Continue to think about ways you can practice demonstrating self-respect.

Take stock of values. Assess the values most important to you. Ensure that these values are upheld in your life and are reflected in what you expect and allow from others.

Don't over-sacrifice. Watch out for the tendency to sacrifice your own needs or well-being as you give in to others. Doing so reinforces messages and feelings that cause low self-esteem to endure. Beware of people-pleasing and the desire to gain approval and acceptance, as self-esteem cannot be built through external validation.

Replace negative self-talk. Pay attention to distorted thinking and negative self-talk that prevents you from acting in ways that demonstrate self-respect. Change negative self-talk with positive affirmations and thoughts.

Practice assertiveness skills. It will help you to act with confidence and self-respect during moments of decision or conflict. As you learn to trust yourself, allow your instincts to guide you.

Choose healthy spaces. Make an effort to avoid people and situations that make it difficult for you to feel good or act in self-respecting ways.

Make time for self-care. Continue to practice affirmations, healthy self-talk, and being kind to yourself. Add to your list of affirmations new statements that focus on self-respect and assertiveness.

Keep your promises. As you continue working toward improved self-esteem, stay true to your promise to make positive changes and implement the recommendations you learn in these steps.

Choose one value that is important to you and focus on ways you can uphold that value in every interaction you encounter this week. Write your name in your calendar or day planner as you schedule a time for yourself. Turn down one obligatory request or invitation in the next few weeks and write about how that makes you feel. Practice expressing an opinion or making a request in a low-conflict situation.

When you have a solid grasp of who you are today, where you have come from, and what experiences have impacted your self-image, you can move toward improved self-esteem. Self-awareness allows you to identify where you lack self-esteem, understand exactly how low self-esteem negatively impacts your life, and, importantly, make changes to improve self-esteem. You are getting in touch with who you are, and the process can be transformative. From there, you can begin taking ownership of your life and readily understand and change any negative aspects that may have contributed to low self-esteem.

Chapter 3
Romantic Love: Love Only Those You Value

T The relationship between romantic relationships and self-esteem has been the focal point of many studies.

Understanding Relationships and Make the Most of Them

Relationships can be tricky. If you are in a romantic relationship, it is often hard to know how to make the most of it. When you try to understand your partner, you will better understand how they will react and why. You may not read social cues well with an introverted temperament, making you struggle in relationships, both romantic and non-romantic.

Here are some techniques to guide you in making the most out of the relationships in your life. Some tips apply to romantic relationships and partnerships, and others apply to non-romantic relationships and friendships.

<u>Think positive thoughts</u>: Try not to dwell on the negativity that life throws your way. Practicing a positive mindset will benefit you in your relationships. Keep in mind that you don't want someone focusing on the negativity you bring to a relationship, so strive to be positive. Thinking positive is the best way to begin!

<u>Argue healthily</u>—set ground rules for when you argue. People will disagree regardless of how healthy the relationship is. Having boundaries about what is fair and not fair in an argument is important to retain the relationships even after the argument is over.

<u>Don't fight about money</u>. If you can avoid the money fight, your relationship will benefit. Money is usually the vast cause of stress and arguments in relationships. Your romantic relationships will be stronger than ever because of it. Use words of encouragement. Everyone can benefit from encouragement, but your partner especially can. When you strive to use words that encourage and build up, you invest in the other person rather than words that tear down.

Characteristics of a Healthy Relationship

When you look at your relationships, both romantic and non-romantic, it is important to know the nature of a healthy relationship. The common characteristics that both include are:

<u>Respect</u>: respecting each other in your relationship is important. When you honor the other person and care about what that person wants, you respect your partner.

<u>Security and Comfort</u>: security and comfort in a relationship will give you stability and make you feel confident that the relationship is a positive aspect of your life.

<u>Nonviolence:</u> relationships are nonviolent, and they should never enter a violent phase. Please seek help and leave the person if you are in a violent relationship.

<u>Resolve conflict</u>: the ability of two people to resolve conflict easily is important in a relationship. How you resolve conflict determines the level of respect in your relationship.

<u>Enjoy each other:</u> enjoying the other person in a relationship is important. You should enjoy spending time together and listening to the other person talk. If you don't, or that person doesn't seem to have that same level of enjoyment for you, the relationship is probably not healthy.

<u>Support one another</u>: supporting one another makes a relationship stable. You may not always agree, but offering your support to others' ideas and goals is important.

<u>Interested in the other person's life</u>: take an interest in the other person's life and know what they want from it. When you pay attention to their ideas, their goals, and their aspirations, you look at the person as a whole, and you show love.

<u>Privacy and confidence</u>: when you have confidence that what you tell a person will remain private, you build a healthy relationship.

Trust: you must trust the person you are in a relationship with. If you cannot, the relationship is not healthy.

<u>Clear and open communication</u>: honest and clear lines of communication are essential in a relationship. You must be able to talk to each other and not fear being misunderstood.

<u>Encourage friendships</u>: when you encourage other friendships outside of your relationship, you give the other person freedom to be who they are and enjoy others who with the same interests and goals.

<u>Honesty</u>: honesty is important in a relationship, whether a romantic or a non-romantic relationship. When you can be honest with the other person, you know that you are valued and safe.

How Self-Esteem Impacts Relationships

How you deal with yourself lays the groundwork for every other relationship in your life. Self-esteem allows us to have healthy relationships with our partners, family, friends, and other significant people in our lives. Our self-esteem is not an unmoving entity that exists in a vacuum—rather, it intersects with other people and their respective levels of self-esteem, too. The repercussions of relationships that involve low self-esteem with one or both people can be astounding.

Research shows that highly self-critical people tend to be dissatisfied in their relationships. They judge themselves and assume others judge them just as harshly, thus displaying oversensitivity and defensiveness in their interactions. It undermines closeness , preventing trust, intimacy, and effective communication instead of creating distance, loneliness, and a lack of support that threatens self-love.

With low self-esteem, you may inadvertently act in ways that negatively impact healthy and otherwise stable relationships, creating a vicious cycle where low self-esteem and relationship dysfunction reinforce one another. Low self-esteem consequences in a relationship involve constantly feeling like a victim, being passive or aggressive, acting in needy or clingy ways, or testing (and ultimately sabotaging) positive relationships. Any of these behaviors have the potential to ruin relationships, leaving you feeling isolated and alone.

Low self-esteem also increases your susceptibility to forming unhealthy relationships. Without healthy self-esteem, you may rely too much on others, allowing them to assume all the power. It increases your vulnerability of being taken advantage of, succumbing to peer pressure, or finding yourself stuck in relationships that involve patterns of abuse.

As you think about your self-esteem and your interactions with the people in your life, reflect on whether you engage in behaviors that prevent you from having healthy relationships. It may help to look back over your responses to the Low Self-Esteem Checklist. Did you check anything that might contribute to problematic exchanges in your relationships? If so, consider what it would take to make changes to decrease or end these behaviors. Think about how loving you will change your relationships for the better. In the space provided, write about the differences and benefits the people in your life will experience from your learning to love yourself.

How Can We Use Our Emotions to Our Advantage?

The first step in using your emotions to your advantage is learning how to control them. By learning how to control our emotions, we are learning how to manipulate the situations around us. When we control the situations around us, stress and anxiety will be reduced.

<u>Don't react right away</u>. When you delay reaction, you give yourself the gift of re-evaluating the situation rather than possibly reacting inappropriately.

<u>Find a healthy outlet</u>. If you are suffering from strong emotions such as anger, find a way to expend the anger that will not cause damage to your relationships.

<u>See the bigger picture</u>. Look at the bigger aspect of the situation. When you focus on the bigger picture, you will often lose steam with strong emotions.

<u>Reframe your thoughts</u>. Changing your perspective will help you decide if you are reacting appropriately or not. Understand your emotional triggers. Being attuned to your emotions allows you to understand what triggers you. If politics make you angry, avoid them when it is not appropriate to get heated. Knowing that you become sad during sappy movies helps you avoid them to save face.

<u>Strive for self-awareness</u>. Become aware of who you are at your core.

<u>Practice self-awareness and self-help.</u> This allows you to know what you like, what you don't like, and how to proceed from there.

How Being Positive Will Help You Succeed - and More

Living an optimist's life can benefit you in more than one way. You may not perceive it at first, but it is an amazing difference from having negative thoughts—like night and day.

Practicing optimistic self-talk is the ability to respond to the pessimistic thoughts that come to mind. It also makes you manage your thoughts better and will get better through constant practice.

Staying positive is not a piece of cake. It will need practice like everything else. Baby steps have to be taken, but after gradual practice, you'll soon get the hang of it.

Positivity results in doing simple things. It's so simple that you'll wonder why you haven't done it as soon as you could. About the cloud with silver lining. It's true. Yes, it sounds like an endless cliché, but seeing the positive side in any situation would help more. A bad situation still has a good side.

Difficult situations can be viewed as a challenge and a way to grow and be a better individual. Encountering loss can be viewed as a reminder of the things important to you and further appreciate the things you currently have. Enjoy life's simple pleasures. Every event can be celebrated and enjoyed.

Have you encountered a difficult day in the office? Look at it as an opportunity to have a get-together afterward. Are you doing chores? Look at it as a chance to do some thinking and meditation and as a way to burn calories if you're trying to lose weight. Note the small things in life and realize how each of them can be an opportunity for enjoyment. Look at yourself, and even at others, in a positive way. There's a good side in each individual; you just have to realize it.

Let Go of Your Fears

Fear is normal. Do not feel ashamed for feeling afraid. Every person in this world is afraid of something. You may ask why then you are being asked to let go of it if it is normal. A person with a negative outlook spends their life worrying about destructive fears. Fear is a damaging emotion, especially when it becomes a part of your daily habits and takes over your life.

Being fearful makes a person paralyzed. It inhibits them from doing even the simplest task. They spend their life worrying about and anticipating a bad thing that is yet to happen (if it will happen at all). Lingering on their anxiety will consequently get them nowhere.

Most of the time, fear is motivated by the desire of something so bad that it makes a person anticipate the worst because they believe they will prevent the bad from happening if they focus on what might go wrong. But it never works out that way. Wasting too much time and energy worrying instead of doing something about it is not a good idea. It consumes you so much that it takes away the positivity in your desire.

On the other hand, a fear channeled in a positive light can serve a greater purpose; it can be a person's driving force.

39

Chapter 4
The Virtue of Excellence

Perfectionism has acquired several meanings in contemporary moral and political philosophy. Generally speaking, perfectionist writers advance an objective account of the good and then develop an account of ethics and because it identifies states of affairs, activities, among others.

Both men and women who make destructive or self-deprecating decisions that demonstrate a lack of self-respect stay trapped in a cycle of low self-esteem. When you fail to make healthy changes, act in self-denying ways or make poor choices, this inevitably leads to negative self-talk that further depletes self-esteem. In this case, you have to work twice as hard to block negative messages as you find a way to rationalize your actions, inactions, or self-destructive decisions. When you make bad decisions that harm yourself or others, you feel bad about who you are and feel out of control, making healthy self-esteem very difficult.

Can you think of any bad decisions you've made or regrets you have had? While it may be difficult to reflect on past choices (especially if you regret them!), considering past behaviors is a helpful first step to building up self-respect. Based on these reflections, you can determine your core values and maintain the discipline (and self-respect!) necessary to ensure that your values stay in line. Learning how to respect yourself also involves looking at ways you honor or discredit yourself. Think of it this way: when we make choices and act in ways aligned with healthy values and self-nurturing goals, we feel good about ourselves and better build and maintain self-esteem.

Perfection is Driving You Crazy

Often one of the biggest roadblocks to your self-esteem is expecting everything to be perfect all of the time. You want the presentation to be perfect, your life to be perfect, and everyone to think you are perfect. You may spend hours trying to get things right, only to feel frustrated the moment things go wrong. And they are going to go wrong. Those who expect perfection are often disappointed when life naturally goes wrong.

Recognize When Standards are Unreachable

Everyone should have goals in their life. They should have some standard that they want to reach in their lives. Otherwise, what are you working for? But there is a difference between obtainable goals and those that you may never achieve. For example, making a goal to lose 40 pounds in a month is not very reasonable, but aiming for a few pounds each week can be a great place to start.

Concentrating on the wrong kinds of goals can be a major blow to your self-esteem because they will cause you to feel like a failure when you cannot reach them. When you set unobtainable goals, you are setting yourself up for failure. These goals are too hard for you or anyone else to reach in the amount of time you specify. You will not be able to reach the result, no matter how hard you try. It leads you to feel down and depressed because you failed; it doesn't matter that the goal was unreachable in the first place. When you continuously set yourself up for failure, you will never feel confident because you never succeed.

So rather than setting you up in this way, you need to start going with more obtainable goals. It does not mean set up easy goals, and you can accomplish them in one day. These won't bring you a lot of satisfaction, and you will get bored with them pretty quickly. Rather, you need to pick some that will be a bit of a challenge, you will need to work a bit to reach them, but you will reach them if you put in the hard work.

With the obtainable goals, you are going to feel so amazing when you do reach the end. You will look back and see how hard you worked, how you kept on going with the hard work, and how great it felt to be at the end finally. It will help your self-esteem soar because you know you can accomplish anything you put your mind to.

Try Your Best

There may be a difficult project at work that you are unsure about, you may have a parenting challenge, or many other things may come up that make you wonder if you will get the work done. When the challenges occur, you may feel like it is impossible to get it all done. You will want to give up or feel your confidence plummet when you start feeling this way.

Instead of feeling like you won't do the challenge perfectly, just try to do it your best. Get to work and tackle the challenge in the best way your know-how. All challenges are sent your way for a reason, as when the boss thinks you have the best time management skills. The final project may not be perfect, but you will feel great for a job well done when you do your best and concentrate on working hard.

Forgive When Things Mess Up

When you make a mistake, you just need to forgive yourself and move on. Holding onto the mistakes you made will make you miserable. You will focus all your energy on this mistake, letting it take over your mind and your happiness. Rather than focusing on everything you have done right, you will spend time thinking about the one thing you did wrong.

It is going to make you feel miserable. Things happen, and it is much better to focus on the good in your life than the few things that don't go right. Other people don't look at you and see all the mistakes. They look at you and see a good friend, a great speaker, someone who is always there for them, or the other great things that make you special to them. If other people don't see the mistakes, why should you spend so much time and energy on them? Realize that the mistake was made and correct it the best way possible. Once that is done, move on and concentrate on all the good things you have done in life. And there are plenty. You are a wonderful person who just needs to show everyone else you're magic, and you will feel so much happier when you concentrate on the good and forget the bad.

You may fear that acting in your own best interest or speaking up will lead to conflict, including judgment, anger, or hurt feelings of others, or it may create vulnerability, opening you up to potentially appear selfish or ignorant. Do you ever hesitate to say no to things and wind up overextending yourself? Distorted thinking and fear also lead to people-pleasing behaviors. Fear of failure, disappointing others, or being criticized or rejected gets in the way of making healthy choices that foster individual well-being.

The problem is that giving away your power and diminishing your value by failing to extend the same respect and attention toward your own needs results in more distorted thinking around your worth. Also, attempting to gain worth or significance from pleasing others can lead to burnout or feelings of resentment or devastation when your help and sacrifices aren't appreciated. Complete the following assessment to determine where you stand concerning people-pleasing. As you do so, consider all of your relationships, including those with family, friends, coworkers, and even strangers.

A choice is a very important factor when reshaping and restructuring thoughts. When we choose to think positively, we are restructuring, recalibrating, and reshaping our brains, the neurons inside, and the thought patterns and habits that affect daily life. As you are aware, our thoughts profoundly influence everything, our inner world and internal health, and our outer environment. So, shifting perspectives to those more in alignment and harmony with a reality rooted in love, positivity, unity, connection, abundance, bliss, new opportunities, experiences, and anything else associated with a positive, healthy mindset actively influences the focus of our awareness.

Realize Mistakes Happen

Mistakes are going to happen during your life. Nothing is going to end up perfectly the way that you would like. People aren't going to act in the way that you would like. You won't be able to take on all the work that you would like all the time; things are going to get in the way, and no matter how hard you try, and mistakes are going to occur. The more you worry about the project, hoping that it turns out perfect, the more mistakes will occur.

It just brings you a lot of stress, and when things don't work out the way you would like, you will assume that you did something wrong. It can be a big hit to your overall confidence level, and it can take a long time to build it back up. Those who expect perfection will be hit the hardest when they realize a mistake has occurred.

So, instead of adding all this stress to your life and feeling that everything has to be perfect, take a step back and breathe. Mistakes will happen, and realizing this when you start can help you take it easy. It does not mean you shouldn't take the work seriously, but when you realize that you aren't perfect, you can approach the project differently and are less likely to make a mistake. Mistakes are going to happen, but try your hardest, and you will do a great job.

Everyone would like perfection in their lives. They would like to impress everyone they come across and do a great job with every project. While this is a great idea to reach, no one is going to reach perfection each time. Expecting to get to perfection can make things impossible in your life; you will find that when you have this frame of mind, rather than taking it easy, mistakes will hit you the hardest. Learning how to accept perfectionism and try your hardest on each project, and you will find that your self-esteem can soar.

Ditching "Have" for "Get"

Another example is positive language, and using that language to make sure you control your thinking is just a minor shift. Whenever you can, eliminate the use of the word "have to" when you are talking about an obligation. Instead of having to do something, phrase it as you "get to" do something. This little shift will have a huge, profound effect when you make use of it regularly. All you have to do is change up how you speak to yourself, and you will discover that your general attitude alters for the better.

Chapter 5
Respect Your Body with Exercise

Exercising More Frequently

Exercising is an essential part of our everyday lives that many of us tend to overlook. When we do not exercise adequately, we experience the effects both physically and mentally. Physically, we struggle to do things that might have been easy for us at one point. Perhaps we feel like we are not on par with our peers. It can be more of a challenge to carrying out things, enjoy doing activities with loved ones, or otherwise stay active and involved in others' lives when struggling with ill health due to lack of exercise. Low stamina and increased chronic pain are just two of the many things that people with a poor exercise routine face.

Exercising does not need to be an extensive, hard-core workout that consumes all your time. Going for a brisk walk each day, spending a few minutes at the gym, or even doing a home workout routine in your living room are all great choices. If you are unable to work out due to a physical disability or preexisting health condition, consider communicating with your doctor to see what forms of exercise you may be able to engage in that will help you feel better. There may be smaller and lower-impact things you can do such as yoga or light stretching.

The key here is not to outdo yourself or compete with anyone. The key, instead, is to support yourself in achieving the best health possible. As a result, you will begin to feel significantly better both physically and mentally.

How Practicing Meditation Helps Build Self–Esteem

Besides, it significantly improves every aspect of your physical and emotional health. Many meditation techniques are beneficial, as they involve eliminating every thought going through your head. Clearing your mind by getting rid of negative thoughts will help restart your mind and allow it to be more relaxed, enabling you to think more clearly and rationally.

As mentioned earlier in the book, it's important to remember that negative thoughts that filter through during meditation are not abnormal, and it doesn't mean that you're doing it wrong! Instead, focus on not engaging with those thoughts. Instead of allowing anxiety, criticisms, and worries to have space in your head, simply let those thoughts pass. If you find yourself too fixated on something to meditate on, try to refocus your mind on your breathing. Focus on the way breathing forces your chest to expand and collapse. Notice how you physically feel doing the meditation. Don't let negativity invade this space for long!

Practicing mindfulness meditation techniques has been shown to have a wide variety of incredible benefits for overall health! It has the power to improve all aspects of your physical and emotional health, benefitting you as a whole. Here are some excellent reasons why you should start practicing mindfulness meditation today! Meditation has been shown to reduce chronic pain, lower blood pressure, and alleviate a wide array of gastrointestinal issues.

It also improves sleep, decreases insomnia, helps treat heart disease and stress. Mindfulness meditation also enhances an array of mental/emotional aspects of your health. For instance, it helps treat depression, reduce obsessive-compulsive behaviors, anxiety, relationship conflicts, stress and irritability, and negative thought patterns associated with eating disorders. It further functions as a significant element in treating substance abuse.

Meditation has also been shown to increase brain function and the grey matter found in part of the brain related to self-control and attention. Another clear benefit of meditation is that it has also been proven to regulate the part of the brain that produces stress hormones (cortisol), reducing stress.

Mindfulness meditation has many favorable advantages that lead to a plethora of improvements and enhancements in virtually every aspect of your physical and emotional health. It has the incredible power to improve immunity while creating positive brain changes, lower stress, and assist in coping with chronic health issues such as chronic pain, cancer, and heart disease, only to name a few. A recent meta-analysis of 20 empirical reports has shown plenty of evidence that mindfulness meditation drastically increased physical and mental well-being in battling heart disease, chronic pain, cancer, and autoimmune disorders.

Integrative body-mind training has also been shown to be linked with improved axonal density, the signaling connections in our brain. This handy little meditation technique also leads to increased protective tissue, or myelin, around the axons in the anterior cingulate brain region. Many experts believe that one of the prominently important ways how mindfulness meditation works is by improving peoples' ability to accept their experiences (including painful and unpleasant emotions that are associated with difficult experiences and situations) rather than immediately react to them negatively: with resentment, fear, anger, bitterness, aversion, and avoidance. The wonderful thing about practicing mindfulness meditation is that it heals and improves our mental/emotional state by causing us to view life from a much more transparent, wiser, more rational, and healthier perspective.

It's becoming more common for mindfulness meditation to be combined with psychotherapy, particularly cognitive-behavioral therapy. This development in psychotherapy makes clear and perfect sense, as meditation and cognitive behavioral therapy

share the same goal of helping people gain awareness, understanding, and a better perspective on maladaptive, destructive,
irrational, and self–defeating thought patterns.

Meditation Helps You Become a Better Person

Mindfulness has a virtuous effect on us, causing us to be more
compassionate, which benefits the people we interact with! Researchers from Harvard and Northwestern Universities discovered that meditation, particularly mindfulness, is strongly linked
with increased patterns of virtuous, "do-good" behavior. Who
would've thought!

Meditation Helps Support Weight–Loss!

In a study, the participants consumed a significantly reduced ca-
loric intake than those who didn't engage in mindful eating, even
though they were hungrier than the opposing control group! It led
the mindful eaters to lose more weight in the long run and acquire
a new appreciation for healthier foods. The study shows that this
will lead to developing long-term healthy eating patterns to maintain a healthy weight in the long run.

Breathing Method

Begin by finding a quiet, peaceful, and distraction-free place. Now
with your back straight. Relax, focus, and feel each sensation that
comes with each breath you take as it slowly moves in and out of

your body. Let your distracting thoughts of everything else disappear, and just direct your focus on breathing. Pay attention to your nostrils as the air moves in and out. Notice how your abdomen expands and then collapses with each breath. When your mind begins to wander, stop and gently redirect your undivided attention to your breath. Don't judge yourself. Keep in mind that you're not trying to beat or master anything — such as becoming a skilled meditator, as this isn't a race to perfection. You're simply eliminating all your thoughts and, instead, becoming in touch and aware of all the simple little details involved in what's happening around you, breath by breath.

Progressive Muscle Relaxation Meditation Technique

Before practicing this exercise, make sure you consult with your doctor if you suffer from any physical complications, including muscle spasms, back or neck problems, or other injuries or muscle conditions that can be potentially aggravated by tensing your muscles. Start by getting comfortable. Remove your shoes and change into comfortable clothing. Now that you're dressed comfortably, take a few minutes just to relax and take nice and slow deep breaths. Inhale and exhale.

Next, start to slowly tense your right foot muscles while squeezing as tightly as you possibly can. Do this for 10 seconds. If you like, you can count to 10 out loud. Now move onto your right foot, relax and direct your full focus on the tension that's flowing away from your foot and how it feels as it becomes relaxed.

Stay in this peaceful and relaxed state for a few moments while slowly and calmly taking deep breaths. Inhale and exhale. When you're ready to move on, direct your entire focus onto your left foot. Now repeat the same muscle tension and release process, the same way you did on your right foot. Move slowly upwards throughout your whole body, contracting and relaxing the various muscle groups as you go. It may take some practice and discipline at first but try not to tense your muscles for longer than 10 seconds.

Walking

This incredibly healthy practice works wonders on clearing your mind and helping you cope with overwhelming emotions, including grief. For this exercise, start by first finding a space outside and simply start walking at a slow to medium pace while focusing on your feet. Try to pay close attention to when your toes touch the ground, when your foot is flat and pressing against the floor and when your toe points back in an upward position. Now, feel the foot roll, paying close attention to every sensation, and noticing each sensory detail whether you feel an itch, a pull of the sock, or how your foot feels against the ground.

When feeling your mind beginning to wander into the chaotic land of scattered thoughts (it will probably be, and it's completely normal), shut off your mind and gently proceed to bring your attention back to your feet after you've eliminated all other thoughts. With this exercise, you're practicing and building the vital skill of being aware when your concentration begins drifting into default mode. At the same time, you'll also be training yourself to bring it back into focus.

Building and strengthening this skill will effectively help you be more present in the moment and more in control of your thoughts and attention every day, and it will be particularly useful in times of stress when our minds tend to wander most. With the skill, you'll be more in touch with your thought patterns while knowing what your brains up to. It will help you immediately identify the negative thought patterns associated with low self-esteem. In that way, you can stop them and shift to a more positive place in your mind.

This exercise can be so beneficial and rewarding that you should dedicate a specific time and chosen location to practice it. When you have become more comfortable with walking meditation, try taking it to the next level by practicing as you're walking to the bus stop, office, classroom, grocery store, or just about anywhere you please.

Engaging in mindful meditation techniques is beneficial to all aspects of your body, both physically and emotionally. In fact they will also offer favorable improvements to every aspect of your life, including relationships, family situations, and work. You will realize the positive benefits they offer to counter the typical stress, negativity, and inconvenience.

Chapter 6
Be Kind to Yourself

When you struggle with self-esteem regularly, it can be challenging to believe in any positive feedback about yourself. That is because, while you need this type of feedback, you are stressed out further when someone compliments you or tries to let you know that you are doing something right. You start to feel pressured to perform at a higher level, which is a struggle for you since you do not feel you can be successful or provide beneficial support to others.

Suppose you have been struggling with low self-esteem for some time. In this case, it may be wise to forego the effort to improve self-esteem on your own and find a professional who can assist you with the struggle you are currently in to feel better about yourself.

Setting the Right Goals

While we have mentioned goals to follow, it won't harm anyone if you set goals for yourself. There is no harm whatsoever in planning the process at your own pace. However, we believe that setting goals is a process that shouldn't be taken lightly. The goals you set define how appreciated you feel and how you can achieve the objectives you have in mind. If you aren't dedicated to your goals, you will never achieve the success you crave. It is usual for people to have self-esteem waves, where they are either comfortable with their attitude toward life or not comfortable.

We are here to guide you in self-esteem management, including setting goals, as you need to perceive how essential it is for you to set the right goals going forward. Setting goals is an essential part of having a healthy and growing self-esteem. To set your goals the right way, both men and women need to follow the SMART criteria. The SMART criterion is a successful method that will help you become clear with your goals and achieve them in the best manner possible. To follow the smart criteria, you need to keep in mind what it entails and how it can help you move forward with your goals.

The 5 SMART criteria boast acronyms for the following words: Specific, Measurable, Achievable, Relevant, and Timely. We will learn all of these factors in greater detail below to help you out in this process:

1. Specific

What exactly are you looking to achieve? The more detailed you are with the dream, the better you will be able to achieve it. To achieve higher self-esteem is your ultimate goal, but what methods do you want to employ to achieve that landmark? To be specific with your goals, you need to break them down to achieve your desired results.

For instance, a goal that isn't specific would say "I want to improve my self-confidence," while a specific goal would say "I want to improve my self-esteem by focusing on positive thinking for the next six months."

2.   Measurable

Once you're sure that the goal you're setting for yourself is specific, go on to check whether it is measurable or not. By measurable, we mean that you should identify the progress you're making and be able to see, feel, and hear when you eventually reach the end goal you have in mind.

Since self-esteem is an attitude and a process of the mind, you surely cannot see or hear it, but you can feel it. So, it is all about being honest to yourself and tracking the progress you feel during the period you're vying to get to the top.

You can break your goals down into measurable thoughts. For instance, if you want to reach the ultimate goal of no negative thoughts, you need to reach a stage where you stop bowing down to negative thoughts. You should identify a negative thought whenever it creeps into your mind.

Measurable goals end up going a long way in helping you achieve what you want from your life. You can build your self-esteem by setting quantifiable goals.

3.   Attainable

The "A" in SMART stands for Attainable and is perhaps one of the most important factors to keep in mind while setting goals. The goal you set for yourself should be attainable and easy to achieve.

If a plan isn't accessible or achievable, you will end up wasting a lot of time and effort accomplishing a goal that wasn't possible to achieve at all. A goal that isn't attainable can lead to disappointments in life.

It is perfectly normal to wish for the stars, but if you don't end up achieving what you have in mind, you'll see your aims further slipping away. Smartly planning is a need you should expertly plan for. Don't get blown away by the prospect of brighter results, and always make sure that you remain smart about the objectives that you set for yourself.

4.   Relevant

The goal you set for yourself should be relevant to what you're achieving. It is a crucial point to keep in mind while progressing towards achieving your goals. You cannot seriously set a goal that you have a hard time following upon. The goal you set should be easy to accomplish without any problem as such in the process.

Imagine setting a goal that you effortlessly try to achieve to come but end up seeing that it is not relevant to the end objective. For instance, your objective is to increase your self-esteem. Now, playing guitar every day for the coming six months does not help you in any way towards achieving that objective, so setting that as a goal is pointless.

We discuss possible goals that you can set for yourself in this book, but if you want to set goals for yourself, make sure they are relevant. Knowing the objective behind the goal can often help you in making sure that it is appropriate. Being ambiguous about the objective isn't a desirable practice and can lead you away from achieving the end goal you have your eyes set on.

5. Timely

As is mentioned in the old adage "time is money"; in other words, time is a precious factor in the goal-setting procedure. Deadlines can help you in measuring or tracking your success. Learn how to set deadlines for yourself and make sure you follow them. The timeline or deadline you set should be realistic and easy to follow if you start.

With the tips for goal setting outlined above, you can set your own goals for achieving the objectives you for improving your self-esteem.

Habits You Can Form to Get Started

Starting to work on your self-esteem is something that requires persistent efforts and dedication. You need to be dedicated to the task at hand and should persist with whatever progress you make as part of this effort.

Healthy self-esteem comes from focusing on the small changes you make to your lifestyle. These changes require you to be very honest with yourself so there isn't anything currently lacking in your behavior. Honesty is something you need to be extremely careful about. You cannot seriously expect to witness changes in your self-esteem if you aren't going to be honest to yourself.

You can start the procedure by initiating changes as follows:

Catch Yourself When You Compare Yourself to Others

Comparing yourself to every living thing that breathes can be extremely detrimental to mental health. Not only are you stopping yourself from developing better self-esteem, but you're also pushing down the mental image you have of yourself. It isn't something you would want to do, considering how motivated you are to better your self-esteem and make changes.

People start making comparisons when they feel that they aren't good enough. You should stop comparing yourself to others when you feel you aren't good enough and initiate changes. These comparisons can mess you up and make you feel low about yourself. When you start making changes, you won't feel so low about yourself and think you have an inadequate lifestyle or life choices.

Whenever you compare yourself to someone around you, make sure you negate the comparison by realizing that you are a unique person who brings something special to this world. You're the best version of you so celebrate your uniqueness and rid yourself of those negative thought as soon as possible.

Comparing oneself to others is more often than not followed by sessions of negative self-talk. You feel that you haven't done the right things in life and follow the comparison with a self-bashing session.

Be with Positive People

To witness real mental growth, you need to surround yourself with positive people. Positive people can do wonders to your attitude. As humans, we tend to absorb a lot from the atmosphere we are in. The person you are with can help you a lot with your mental health. If you're with people who continuously demean or remind you of your insecurities, you have minimal possibilities for growth. You need to be wary of the people you are around and work on this to experience growth. Avoid people who especially the absorb the energy around them.

If you're a stay-at-home mom, you don't want negative people around who put you down for your choices. Your choices define you, and you cannot be put down for doing what you deem best for yourself and your children. Healthy self-esteem is about the extrinsic environment we are in more than anything else. People with healthy self-esteem are extrinsically and intrinsically motivated.

Set Realistic Goals

Setting realistic goals can help you a lot when it comes to learning from your mistakes and heading toward your purpose. Goals define the progress you will make in life. You should set that focus on the target, with a follow-up analysis of whether you achieved these goals in the best manner possible.

You need to realize that setting heightened goals not based on reality will push you down rather than pull you up. You would feel even worse about yourself at your inability to accomplish these goals with no progress.

Practice Self-Forgiveness

Self-forgiveness is perhaps one of the best habits you can have when starting to improve your self-esteem. Your self-esteem can take a major hit if you can't forgive yourself for the basic mistakes you have made at some stage of life. Forgive yourself for that relationship that didn't work out; it wasn't entirely your fault. Forgive yourself for feeling irritated after a tiring day, while managing both office and home responsibilities. Forgive yourself for having a cheat day because you were tired. Forgive yourself for wearing a casual look because you were too tired to apply makeup and wear that fancy outfit. You can only experience true self-love when you learn how to forgive yourself.

Chapter 7
Family and Friends Factors

Family and Friends

The people you spend time with have a significant influence on your self-esteem. Your friends can help you develop your self-confidence, a good self-image, and self-respect, or they can abandon you. Unfortunately, individuals in our lives will intentionally try to damage our self-esteem by building themselves up. Your family can also positively or negatively influence your self-esteem. Feelings of inadequacy when with your family can lead to low self-esteem while building and working together as a family can contribute to good self-esteem.

From the day we're born, the people around us convey messages that we internalize to form our core belief system about ourselves and our world. Therefore, it's no surprise that both men and women with unhealthy role models and less nurturing caretakers are be more prone to low self-esteem. Those whose families conveyed that it was not okay to express their feelings can develop identity confusion that leads to low self-esteem problems.

Unfortunately, dysfunction and maladaptive patterns can be passed down for generations. If any of these issues are part of your history, don't be discouraged. By developing an awareness of the problem, you have already taken the first step in breaking that cycle and making lasting improvements.

If you are somebody who grew up with a healthy childhood, you may find yourself wondering where your low self-esteem could have come from. Know that it's not just individuals with troubled backgrounds who struggle with low self-esteem. Even healthy, nurturing families can inadvertently contribute to problems with low self-esteem. Unintentional messages and actions by even the most loving parents can sometimes send messages that create feelings of self-doubt and inadequacy.

For example, a busy parent may unintentionally ignore a child while tending to other responsibilities to support the family. In turn, the child may internalize this lack of attention to mean they are unimportant or not cared about. When a child routinely experiences these types of disappointments, it can hinder the development of healthy self-esteem.

In some cases, family members and others do the best they can, based on their current stressors and upbringing, life experiences, and self-esteem level. However, when we're young or have already formed low self-esteem, we are incapable of seeing things objectively. In this case, others' actions that we interpret as hurtful can create deep-seated internal conflicts that interfere with our identity and self-worth.

The Impact of Family

Think about your history, the experiences you've encountered, and the messages you received in childhood. Look over your responses. Do any of them appear to be factors that could have played a role in hindering healthy self-esteem? Looking at family history can sometimes offer insight into the early origins of problems with low self-esteem and related present-day struggles. You may or may not notice factors in your family history that could have contributed to low self-esteem. Regardless, it is still possible to build self-esteem up, even when the cause is unknown.

Outside Influences

Most research on this subject focuses on how families create legacies of self-criticism and low self-esteem in both men and women. Still, it's not just our immediate families that influence the way we perceive ourselves. Our self-esteem in both childhood and adulthood is also impacted by things we experience in external settings. These experiences can occur within our relationships and what we witness in the world around us. Interactions with teachers, coaches, peers, friends, extended family, and even strangers all can impact self-esteem.

Not surprisingly, things like bullying, abuse, and dealings with narcissistic people create vulnerabilities concerning self-esteem. Additionally, overt or even implied criticism or ridicule by anyone we encounter can make us question our value. As we explored in the past, what we view outside our immediate network in society, can also affect how we feel about ourselves as we equate various expectations with value and worth.

It would be easy to maintain and enhance self-esteem if we were shielded from any external influences. The reality is, everything we experience can impact our self-esteem, whether negatively or positively. As we move through babyhood, our teens, and adulthood, we constantly receive messages about what is considered acceptable and desirable. So, we make comparisons and question whether our own identity fits the bill.

Also, if you are good at self-reflection, you can tell whether a thought is negative or positive as soon as it enters your mind and where it originated. Just when that bad thought creeps into your mind, rubbish it and move onwards. Track your progress. To complicate matters, the same things that challenge our self-esteem can also become challenges in and of themselves when self-esteem is not in a healthy place. Things like dating, working, taking on responsibilities, and interacting with different people open us to new experiences that can shape our self-esteem. If self-esteem is already low, navigating these experiences can be difficult. Without a foundation of healthy self-esteem, even simple interactions can perpetuate doubt about who we are. We continue to interpret and assign negative meaning to our every interaction and internalize this negativity.

As you already know by now, self-esteem is a healthy attitude that can boost your perspective of yourself and the world. You don't want to think low of your worthiness when you realize that everything you want can be achieved through the right measures.

Building healthy self-esteem is a tough task that requires a lot of effort and hard work. Ensure that your self-esteem is on the right side and keep working towards overall improvement. If you feel that you lack self-esteem, start setting goals for yourself. While we could guide you to the achievable goals you can and should set them for yourself. You must perceive how vital it is to focus on your goals and achieve those goals one step at a time – on your own. If you feel that you're falling low on motivation, make sure to remind yourself why you initially started with this journey.

Support Network

With healthy self-esteem, it's easier to identify the important relationships and components in your network. You can keep supportive, encouraging, and uplifting people and experiences in your micro-network while keeping toxic, unhealthy, or more demanding relationships on the periphery. As you work toward building healthier self-esteem, pay attention to the various relationships you identified in your network. Think about who makes you happy and builds you up. Think about who and depletes your energy or brings you down.

The ideal goal is to maintain at least a handful of very close connections in your micro-network. Whether they're family members, close friends, or trusted mentors, these are the people who appreciate you and have your best interest at heart. If you don't have good connections in your network, consider making the effort to meet new people by pursuing new activities or joining new organizations. We will explore relationships and setting boundaries more in future steps. For now here are some things to do:

<u>Purge the negativity</u>. Continue to practice catching negative self-talk and work to reframe any self-deprecating messages into rational statements that reinforce your value.

<u>Utilize affirmations</u>. Give yourself praise and encouragement. Be your cheerleader and create rituals and routines that incorporate affirmations daily. You'll reprogram your brain as a result of the practice of establishing this new habit.

<u>Beware of self-doubt</u>. Take small risks and challenge yourself to try new things. Remember that building self-esteem takes a series of baby steps. Sometimes it may feel like you are not going anywhere as you work to banish your inner critic and feel deserving of good, but keep pushing forward.

<u>Adopt self-care basics</u>. Concentrate on exercising, sleep, healthy eating, and consider the motivating factors as you set realistic

goals. Work to find balance and establish a sense of well-being by taking time out every day for self-care.

Lower Risk of Depression

When you are a positive person, there is a much better chance that you can stave off depression. Here is how:

Learn to be resistant to stress

Stress is not nearly as much of a problem for those that are positive thinkers. That is not to say that they never feel stressed out at all, but rather, they can resist that stress for far longer than those around them. They can keep from becoming overwhelmed by that negativity or stress in their lives, which matters greatly.

Learn how to be happier

Usually, those that think positively are also able to maintain a happier lifestyle. They are typically able to discover that they are far more likely to find enjoyment from the world around them because they can think about things without having them weighed down by negativity.

Better Immune System

It has been found that people with better mindsets also have better immune systems as well. When you can keep your thinking and feelings positive, you can usually help yourself have a better immune system rather than not having a good one at all. You will get sick less often, and you are more likely to recover from common ailments like the cold sooner.

Better Wellbeing

You will generally have better well-being when you can remain positive in your thinking. When it comes right down to it, positivity is linked to better mindsets and better lifestyles, all of which can then be linked to living a healthier life.

Better Relationships

It has been found that marriages require the use of positivity. It is no surprise but, on average, the magic number is a ratio of 5 to 1. When you have five positive interactions for every negative one, you are much more likely to have a better life and better marriage. When that ratio gets lower, you will find that the marriage is more likely to fail.

Better Success Rates in Jobs

When you think positively, you are much more likely to be successful at work. Your positive work experience is going to be, on average, much more successful than negative ones. In particular, jobs that involve interactions with other people are highly benefitted by adding positivity to those interactions.

Living Longer

It has been found that for people who live positive lifestyles, life expectancy increases.

More Friends and a Better Social Life

Positive people usually also bring with them more friendships, which usually leads to more happiness. When you can maintain that positivity and those better relationships with your friends and family, you will see that you are happier in general—and positivity will aid you here.

Strive for these things, fight depression and negative self-talk and keep a poor self-image at bay.

Chapter 8
Shaping Your Self-Esteem

Early Messages that Shape Self-Esteem

A great gift is being able to explore a greater awareness of who you are and how your past shaped your current level of self-esteem. It will evoke the messages you may have internalized while growing up. As you read through the following list of messages, check the boxes for any items that stand out as true for you.

These do not have to be messages heard aloud; they might be things you interpreted based on what you observed, encountered, or experienced. Don't become overly involved in logic or reasoning; check what resonates with you emotionally. Do not forget that you may have received mixed messages or different messages from different individuals at different times in your entire life, so it's perfectly fine to check two messages that seem like opposites.

Self-Talk and Self-Criticism

The messages we receive and internalize in childhood become a part of our view of ourselves and contribute to the tone of our inner voice or what is frequently referred to as self-talk. Our self-talk is comprised of everything we think throughout our day, both consciously and subconsciously. All day, we think things to ourselves—we give ourselves feedback, reflect upon various encounters, and contemplate details of past, present, and future endeavors.

It may be difficult to identify thoughts or put them on paper because we aren't used to paying close attention to our thoughts or forming thoughts into complete words and sentences. But even when specific thoughts are not at the forefront of our minds, we are still thinking. You may be focused on the words you are reading, yet a part of your mind is still thinking and processing information about whether you agree with what you read, whether it makes sense, or how you may be able to relate to what you are learning.

You may be thinking, "This feels ridiculous" or "I don't think I'm thinking anything." But those thoughts are exactly what I'm talking about. It's your inner dialogue and the flurry of thoughts on your mind that make up self-talk. Some people describe self-talk as "a little voice" in their mind, and if you're not typically reflective, you might admit that recognizing it makes you feel a little crazy; but in reality, self-talk is a very normal thing. We all engaged in something, and it's not the same thing as being delusional or having schizophrenia. It is just a part of human existence and having an evolved brain—and for the record, it can be a wonderful gift to have. Your conscience, your values, your intuition—

they are all tied to self-talk. Developing your self-talk awareness is an important step in getting to know yourself and becoming more conscientious about how you think. Self-Talk and Early

Messages

Self-talk is often shaped by the messages we hear or infer growing up, sometimes even directly reflecting the voices we heard as children. Suppose you routinely received or sensed criticisms from others. In that case, you are more prone to have developed a strong, critical inner voice that echoes the judgment you encountered—or continue to encounter—from other people. As you begin listening to your inner voice, pay attention to the times when that self-talk seems to reflect or mimic the messages you received or believed about yourself earlier in life.

Self-Esteem and Negative Self-Talk

Both men and women with low self-esteem typically have patterns of thinking that are habitually negative, especially regarding thoughts that are personal and self-focused. If it gets out of hand, self-talk can be like an internal critic that judges our every move. The internal critic for those with low self-esteem tends to be overly judgmental and extremely self-belittling. If you have low self-esteem, you likely beat yourself up, second-guess your decisions and harshly criticize your every move through a constant stream of negative self-talk.

The idea behind self-talk is that it's not actual events that control how we feel. It's how we think about an event or situation that determines our moods, emotions, and ultimate action courses. Suzanne became consumed with thoughts of not being good or smart enough. She felt powerless and stayed stuck in a position where she was undervalued and even sexually harassed. On the other hand, Caroline faced the situation with thoughts about how she didn't deserve that type of treatment. She decided to take action and make changes to better her future. Who do you identify with?

Feeling versus Fact

As you dig into who you are, get in touch with your inner voice and explore aspects of your past that contributed to your struggles with self-esteem: it can feel as if your life is a mess. Many men and women identify with every category of distorted thinking and are left feeling like building self-esteem will be a very steep uphill battle. But don't let these feelings discourage you.

While you cannot change your childhood, upbringing, history, or experiences that have led you to where you are today, you can change the way you think and feel about various situations and yourself as a result. You'll learn ways to implement tools and new behaviors to set these changes into motion in future steps. As of now, you are doing vital work, too, just by becoming more aware, identifying what gets in the way of having healthier self-esteem, and looking for any learning opportunity in challenges or set-backs. When you feel overwhelmed or disappointed, ask yourself what the situation taught you or what strengths you have taken away from experience.

Shame and Guilt

Shame and guilt are particularly devastating to both men's and women's self-esteem. When self-esteem is low, you tend to personalize everything that happens, feel guilty, and take responsibility for wrong things. Through negative self-talk, the guilt is transformed to shame, resulting in messages that say, "I did something wrong; therefore, I am bad, I am flawed, I am worthless." Shame is counterproductive to the development of healthy self-esteem, keeping the afflicted trapped in intensely painful feelings and beliefs of worthlessness, isolation, and powerlessness.

Consider these three steps to banishing shame:

1. Communicate with yourself as you would communicate with someone you love.
2. Reach out to someone you trust.
3. Tell your story because shame cannot survive being spoken.

Simply put, empathy is the antidote to shame. In being more compassionate in your self-talk and telling your story to someone you can trust to provide empathy and validation, you can end the powerful destruction of shame and move toward healthy self-esteem.

Rewriting Your Story

Kids are so smart. When they mess up, they simply say, "Do-over!" And they do it over! Well, what's to stop grown-ups from do-overs? All of us are works in progress. We can see ourselves as such and use that mindset to propel us forward with a more positive outlook. As we get wiser with every do-over, we can only get better. As you reflect on the experiences that shaped your current self-esteem level, see if you can rewrite your story to find the silver lining, lessons, or positive takeaways.

You cannot change your history, but you can change the way you feel about past experiences, and you can also control how you talk to yourself about your role in various circumstances. Maybe you were just doing the best you could to survive the chaos, confusion, or dysfunction.

An important part of creating affirmations is to be sure they are written in the first person and the present tense. It gives them more power. It may be a challenge at first. When your self-esteem is low, it can be hard to accept affirmations as true for yourself, and it can be difficult to say them aloud. I tell people to "fake it until you make it." While it may feel ridiculous to talk to yourself using positive affirmations, try it anyway. The more you practice, the less silly it will feel. If you struggle with saying anything to the same effect as the examples provided, try adding the bridge phrase, "I am learning to—I am learning to be well, I am learning to feel I deserve happiness, I am learning to feel worthy, I am learning to feel good enough. I am learning to acknowledge my value."

Next, we will explore goal setting in the areas of diet, exercise, and rest. As you move through these different areas, be realistic with your expectations. Pay close attention to the language you use to set your goals and plans for creating a healthier lifestyle. Remember to continue paying attention to self-talk and watch out for those meddlesome "should" statements that will gear you up for failure instead of encouraging you to move forward in your journey.

Let us start with small goals you can build upon rather than lofty ones that may set you up for disappointment if not achieved.
A healthy body image doesn't mean you look like a model; rather, it means you are generally content with your body the way it is, and you accept that you have positive qualities as well as flaws. Men and women with a healthy body image appreciate their bodies for what they do rather than how they look and recognize that there are greater measures of worth than appearance.

It's perfectly fine to care about appearance—to want to stay fit, enjoy dressing and looking nice, and choose to use makeup and hair products to look your best—but pay particular attention to self-talk around motivation to achieve these things. Are you sending yourself any rigid messages or basing your worth on your ability to live up to unrealistic standards? Or are you able to view body image and appearance as only one aspect of who you are? Rewrite your story with these things in mind!

Look Back to Move Forward

Before we continue, spend some time thinking about the major points of this step and ponder the dictum, Know Yourself, what you have absorbed and how this knowledge has shaped your current view of yourself. Messages we receive or perceive from experiences throughout our lives play a role in our sense of self and how we feel about our identity. These experiences also shape the way we think about, talk to, and treat ourselves.

To build self-esteem, we need to identify our internal dialogue and understand how distorted thinking and unrealistic pressures we place on ourselves impede our ability to experience self-worth. While we cannot change our past facts, we can change our negative self-talk and find meaning that moves us toward acceptance and growth. You may be feeling a variety of things after reading this and delving into your past experiences. SO TAKE ACTION!

Here are some recommended task you can do to reinforce what you've learned.

1. Look back at old family photographs and write about what your life was like as a child.

2. Write down three examples of negative self-talk you caught in your internal dialogue this week. See if you can identify the distortions.

3. Come up with three examples of positive self-talk—or even just one. Write them down and consider how they make you feel.

4. Watch Brené Brown's "Listening to shame" TED Talk (available online).

5. Identify a challenge or setback you encountered this week and see if you can pinpoint one positive lesson from experience.

Chapter 9
Love Yourself

Accepting yourself sets the stage for loving yourself, which is the final step in your journey to obtaining healthy self-esteem. When you can truly love yourself, you become capable of treating yourself with the compassion, flexibility, and affection that are important to maintaining self-esteem throughout life. Loving yourself involves acknowledging and accepting that you deserve love and that others around you benefit from your love, not only your love for them but yourself as well.

The idea of self-love may seem simplistic; however, it's often one of the most difficult steps to achieve for people with low self-esteem, those who have likely suffered years of believing they are not lovable. Truly loving yourself can require hard work and a willingness to be vulnerable, but the rewards are immense. It may feel silly or foreign at first to think about loving yourself but accessing the ability to cultivate self-love has an enormous impact on the path that awaits you beyond this journey. You will learn how to love and protect yourself in ways that will foster healthy self-esteem.

You Deserve Love

It's worth repeating that you possess inherent, unwavering worth as a human. You also have a basic, intrinsic need for love and belonging. We all do. Receiving love, comfort, and support is part of our birthright. Unfortunately, the sense of being unconditionally loved may not have happened for everyone from the start or somehow may have been lost along the way, but the best person to give you the love you need and deserve now is you.

You are the only person who will be there and available for your 100 percent of the time, 24/7, for the rest of your life. Nobody else truly knows the full extent of your history, struggles, tragedies, and triumphs the way you do, so it makes good sense that you strive to be your own best friend rather than your own worst critic.

Demonstrating self-love may be difficult, especially for those who grew up in families where emotions were not expressed. Self-love is accomplished by setting the intention to accept yourself while demonstrating unconditional positive regard for yourself despite anything that comes your way, including weaknesses, flaws, missteps, and imperfections. Consider the unconditional way you would love a child, a pet, or a soul mate and strive to turn that unwavering love inward. Remember that having a healthy self-esteem and exhibiting self-love is not the same as being selfish or arrogant. These things only occur when you disrespect others and care for yourself at the expense of others' well-being.

Celebrating Yourself and Your Progress

Think about and appreciate how complex and miraculous life can be. The fact that a giant tree can sprout from tiny seeds, water, and sunlight is pretty amazing. Regardless of your spiritual, religious, or existential belief system, hopefully, you can see that your existence, too, is remarkable. When you step back and recognize yourself as one unique individual, it may be easier to see yourself through a lens of admiration, in which you can truly celebrate your existence.

Accepting Compliments

You may have found it difficult to give yourself loving feedback, and that's okay. If you are able to write yourself a letter, consider this as an exercise. After you've read it through, you will have gained some experience practicing self-love. If you found writing a love letter to yourself to be challenging, write about what feelings emerged and what got in your way:

Building self-esteem involves learning to be comfortable with receiving compliments—including those from yourself and others. Accepting compliments can be particularly difficult for people with low self-esteem because they do not feel worthy of love and praise. While you may crave compliments and validation, you cannot build self-esteem externally, as we have learned. When self-esteem is low, you are likely to react to compliments with negative self-talk and responses that completely minimize, deny, or discredit the compliment.

When you receive compliments, pay attention to your initial reactions. Do you tend to ignore or dismiss the praise that comes your way? Imagine yourself giving a compliment to someone—a friend, a family member, or a coworker. Imagine what words you might say, then envision how they might react. What would it feel like to be met with resistance or denial?

Practice giving compliments to others this week. Keep track of the five compliments you give and the responses you receive. What do you notice about how people respond to compliments? When we consider it from the other person's angle, it's pretty clear that it's nicer when the person accepts our compliment with a smile and a thank-you. Rejecting compliments not only reinforces low self-esteem but also discredits the person delivering the compliment.

Acknowledging Compliments

Understanding that blocking compliments hampers self-love, pay close attention to any compliments you receive during the next week. You can respect yourself and the opinions and words of others by breaking the habit of deflecting compliments. Instead, work to accept them with grace, allowing them to sink in and respond with a simple thank-you. On the following page, write down any compliments you receive and note whether you felt the urge to discredit them. Write about whether you were able to respond with acceptance. If not, what thoughts or feelings got in the way?

Creating Boundaries

Loving yourself involves distancing yourself from the people in your life who do not respect your welfare and therefore do not deserve your love and attention. People who cannot show you love or treat you in unloving ways are toxic to your growth, well-being, and efforts to build self-esteem. When we love ourselves and have healthy self-esteem, we are less likely to tolerate abusive or unhealthy relationships. Discovering self-love makes it easier to walk away from unhealthy situations and rid ourselves of the toxic people that bring us down.

You have people in your entire life who you cannot escape or completely separate yourself from—perhaps a toxic parent, an abusive family member, an ex with whom you co-parent, or a negative coworker. These boundaries are the rules and limits we set in relationships that guide others to know what we will and will not tolerate. Loving yourself demonstrates a precedent that others will follow.

As you move forward with new relationships, make healthy choices about the people you surround yourself with. Choose people who help support your vision of who you want to be and who empower your self-esteem. Find positive mentors, role models, and friends to make up your emotional support network. Look back at your support network in the exercise you completed. If you do not already have positive, healthy connections in your micro-network, work to establish relationships that meet these criteria.

Volunteering for Yourself

Research has shown that volunteering leads to physical and mental health benefits, including improved self-esteem, especially when volunteering involves helping strangers. Volunteering provides a sense of purpose, chances to interact with others, feelings of belonging, and opportunities to learn new skills, gain new experiences, and develop a sense of achievement. When you choose to volunteer, you demonstrate the conviction that you have something worth offering to others, which in and of itself reinforces your self-esteem.

There are countless ways to volunteer and make a difference in the world and your own life. Look for opportunities in your community at animal shelters, nursing homes, hospitals, homeless or domestic violence shelters, food banks, churches, and local cleanup efforts. List at least five potential volunteer opportunities with phone numbers or websites. Doing so can help contribute to your efforts to build healthy self-esteem.

Compassion for Yourself and Others

Hug yourself! When you treat yourself with compassion and kindness, you are more capable of ensuring that you surround yourself with healthy, loving, and supportive relationships while minimizing your time with people who contaminate your sense of well-being. Simply put, if you look out for yourself like you would a good friend, you're less likely to tolerate people who make you feel negative. Loving and caring for yourself also opens you to be more available to the people you care about. The more compassionate you are about your well-being, the more available you will be to others.

Self-compassion enhances relationships, making them stronger and more gratifying. By loving ourselves, we build self-esteem and decrease our tendency to rely on others to meet our emotional needs and validate our worth. In turn, we become less clingy, needy, and dependent, which enriches the quality of relationships all around. When you start by showing love and compassion toward yourself, you simultaneously become more loving toward others.

You've discovered the importance of love directed toward yourself, from yourself. Hopefully, you've begun the challenge of looking in the mirror, into your own eyes, to express the words, "I love you," or something like it, every day. Although it may feel ridiculous at first, it does get easier with time. Just like you would want to be silly with a best friend, allow yourself to be silly yourself as you take small risks to become stronger.

Engaging in self-love daily practices will help rewire your brain as you develop new ways of thinking and behaving. Self-love is about nurturing your spirit, so practice self-loving actions regularly, just like you care for your mind and body.

As you move forward:

<u>Learn to take a compliment</u>. Be aware of how you react to compliments, demonstrating self-respect and openness to letting love in by choosing to accept kudos with grace.

<u>Fight off doubt.</u> Continue to replace any self-talk doubting your worthiness of praise with positive messages, and create affirmations that support your willingness to hear and speak loving words.

<u>Keep connections positive.</u> Remember that self-love enhances your relationships with others and allows you to maintain healthy and fulfilling connections. Minimize your contact with any abusive people or those who create obstacles to feeling worthy and whole.

<u>Trust in yourself</u>. Use assertiveness to establish and enforce healthy boundaries. Make healthy choices in relationships and interact in ways that support your ability to achieve the best life possible for yourself.

<u>Show compassion</u>. Find ways to express self-compassion and compassion to others through loving actions and willingness to volunteer.

And finally, celebrate your progress as you finish reading this book and contemplate the ways you have grown. Remember that the journey toward loving yourself and improving your self-esteem is an ongoing process that will benefit from continued attention and reflection throughout your entire life.

Chapter 10
Accept Yourself

Once you have made strides in getting to know yourself and have committed to practicing better self-care and treating yourself with respect, the next step is to develop true acceptance of who you are. Accepting yourself involves working a deal with the reality of your humanity, accepting your limits, acknowledging your shortcomings, and recognizing that maintaining healthy self-esteem is a life long journey.

Self-acceptance doesn't happen in a moment; rather, it is an evolution. It involves working through your feelings and dissecting your past experiences to come to appreciate who you are. It's about acknowledging the different traits, experiences, and encounters that make up your existence and coming to terms with the fact that you will have weaknesses. Self-acceptance is about being okay with yourself no matter what has happened or where you are today. Here, you'll learn how to ward off the demons that can sabotage self-esteem as you develop a more secure and forgiving view of yourself.

Acknowledging Limits and Imperfections

One of the biggest challenges to accepting ourselves is recognizing and admitting that we have limits, flaws, and weaknesses. These things are all part of the human experience, yet they can be difficult to accept! Part of building self-esteem involves coming to terms with what these imperfections are and accepting them rather than belittling ourselves for our failure to be perfect.

Eliminating perfectionism is vital to finding self-acceptance. As you move forward, pay attention to the unrealistic goals and expectations you continue to set for yourself; watch out for those times you are pulled toward the unrealistic standards in our society. Also, notice times when you fall into patterns of putting others first, giving away your power, or denying yourself the care and attention you inherently deserve.

Dealing with Criticism

We've already named what to do with negative self-talk and the importance of reframing messages from your inner critic. But how should you handle criticism from others? Dealing with criticism involves another layer of acceptance—acceptance not only that you are imperfect and therefore subject to criticism, but also that the world is a critical place, full of judgment, opinions, and unsolicited feedback.

When self-esteem is low, it's easy to take criticism personally and deplete self-worth feelings further. The trouble is, there will always be criticism, but criticism is not necessarily a bad thing. There are two kinds of criticism: constructive criticism and meant to help move you forward toward growth and development, and criticism that is destructive and meant to cause you humiliation and discomfort. If your self-esteem is low, chances are you react either passively or aggressively to any form of criticism. The problem lies in automatically believing the criticism's validity, allowing it to serve as "proof" that you are damaged and unworthy. It's not the criticism that hurts your self-esteem; rather, it's how you think about the criticism that does the damage. Think of a specific time you received criticism.

The best way to handle criticism is to learn to accept constructive criticism and respond to destructive criticism effectively. Stop and consider whether the criticism is valid and accurate, rather than just accepting it without deliberation. Whether or not the criticism is warranted, you can protect your self-esteem by stopping to take a closer look at the critical message. In doing so, you internalize the message that your point of view matters. Your feelings, opinions, and thoughts are just as important as those of the critic.

If criticism is meant to be constructive and helpful, it's fine to thank the critic for the feedback and move on. If the criticism does not seem valid or warranted, respond in a rational, calm manner, using assertiveness skills to defend your position. You can prepare yourself to handle criticism of any sort with confidence.

Accepting Your Strengths and Weaknesses

Another important aspect of self-acceptance and building self-esteem is knowing your strengths and weaknesses and owning both sides. While strengths are easier to accept, men and women with low self-esteem often have difficulty listing their strengths and find it much easier to pinpoint their weaknesses. Knowing yourself and building self-esteem involves recognizing both.

Think about your strengths, including traits you like, characteristics you are proud of, and the skills and talents you possess. It's important to make an effort to regularly give yourself praise or a pat on the back for the things you do well. Remember that it takes several positives to outweigh a negative, so give yourself ample credit for all of your strengths, using affirmations to acknowledge them and celebrate yourself. List six of your strengths. Write affirmations that show appreciation for these things.

Accepting Your Mistakes

In the past, you identified values that you deem important (here). When self-esteem is low, it can be difficult to uphold these values. We've studied how self-hatred feelings or a desire to escape pain can lead you down a path of making poor decisions that go against your values. These decisions can lead to other bad decisions, like being dishonest and deceitful or engaging in self-destructive behaviors to hide or drown out mistakes. It creates a never-ending cycle of shame that blocks the possibility of building healthy self-esteem. If you find yourself stuck in this type of pattern, take a step back and cut yourself some slack. To find self-acceptance, you will need to acknowledge your actions, accept the mistakes you've made as being just that—mistakes—and move on.

Mistakes are an important part of our experience as humans—we all make them. Mistakes teach us valuable lessons and allow us to learn and grow. Once again, it's how you think about a mistake that dictates how you feel and ultimately determines whether the mistake will hold you back or move you forward.

An important part of self-acceptance involves identifying the negative self-talk that results from any mistake or regret and working to reframe negative messages into kinder, gentler language. Remember to talk to yourself like you would talk to a friend. If you look at each event through a broader, less critical lens, can you see the bigger picture? Can you identify any lessons that can come of this, or at least reframe the situation and decrease negative feelings as a result? When you focus on failures as opportunities for growth and learning, you greatly increase your chances of improving self-esteem rather than condemning yourself.

Knowing Your Threshold for Stress

We all have a certain threshold for stress. When we exceed our capacity to manage stress effectively, we succumb to things like irritability, frustration, anger, fatigue, and desperation in our attempt to cope. Minor issues that would ordinarily be easily managed can put us over the edge when they all pile up at once.

Sometimes, dealing with more major stressors can lead to unhealthy coping strategies and defense mechanisms. Behaviors that may have helped you in the past can become habits and default ways of responding that can get in the way and pose challenges in the present. For example, avoidance may be a current obstacle self-esteem; however, in the past it might have been the only way to survive.

Forgiving Yourself and Others

Part of acceptance may involve a need to forgive, especially when it comes to your shortcomings, mistakes, or personal challenges. Holding grudges and staying stuck in a place of regret, blame, and shame make it difficult to build self-esteem. While acceptance is about coming to terms with a circumstance or event, forgiveness is about processing and ultimately letting go of the feelings of guilt, hurt, anger, and resentment. Part of moving forward toward self-esteem involves letting go of the past and finding forgiveness.

Forgiveness can be a tricky thing. I want to clarify that I do not mean you need to excuse or reconcile with people who have deeply hurt you. Doing so could demonstrate a devaluing of yourself that can inhibit self-esteem even further. Instead, I am talking about accepting that you cannot change others or the events of your past. You can, however, make choices in how you move forward. Choosing to let go of the past, accept what happened, and forgive (especially yourself) allows you to relinquish the past's hold on your life and frees you up to focus on the future.

Forgiveness is not about excusing poor behavior or forgetting something happened, nor is it about minimizing your feelings. It's simply about admitting and accepting things that have happened to move through the feelings and prevent them from keeping you trapped in a place of anger, regret, hurt, or shame.

Steps to forgiveness involve:
- Acknowledging and accepting the reality of what happened
- Allowing yourself to experience and process your negative feelings
- Letting go and moving beyond the negative feelings

Forgiveness is a means of regaining control and taking back your power to find healing. Like much of what we've encountered in this book, forgiveness is a skill that can be learned and practiced. Simply being willing to consider forgiveness opens you up to the mindset that brings about change and the possibility of self-acceptance and self-love. But first, let's find out what needs forgiving.

Letters of Forgiveness

Maybe it's someone else you need to forgive, or maybe it's yourself. Write a letter to the person you most need to forgive. Write stream-of-consciousness style, letting whatever comes up flow onto the paper. Don't worry about spelling, punctuation, grammar, or even making sense. Remember, this experience is just for you, to help you release the past and move toward greater well-being. Once you are finished with the letter, decide what you want to do with it. Feel free to rip up the page and shred or burn it.

Coping with Setbacks

No one has a constant level of healthy self-esteem. Life's challenges can test even the strongest self-esteem. As you work through the steps in this book, you may stay very motivated to move forward toward positive growth, and that's awesome. Working with self-esteem tools can be relatively straightforward when life is going smoothly. But inevitably, life will throw you a curveball that interferes with your remembering to put your skills and tools into action.

Building and maintaining self-esteem is a lifelong process that involves continuous use of the skills and action items presented in this book. Building and maintaining self-esteem often means two steps forward and one step back. Please don't get caught up in anger and frustration at the arrow's life throws your way. Rather, pay attention to the attitude you take during these moments of challenge and draw from this; recognize that you are gaining strength and learning invaluable lessons along the way.

Chapter 11
Signs of Healthy Self-Esteem

What do you think of an individual who always speaks well of others? Do they have high or low self-esteem? You could say that to speak well of others is high self-esteem. You have to think enough about yourself not to be threatened by the excellence of others. On the other hand, you could say that a person who always talks highly about others is a people-pleaser suffering from low self-esteem. So, what is it? A single trait or behavior alone is not a good indicator of self-esteem. That said, here are a few qualities to consider as of signs possible with high self-esteem.

Possible Signs of High Self-Esteem

1. Inviting intimacy. I'm not talking about sex. I'm talking about sharing our authentic selves. Sharing with others is dangerous if we are afraid of not doing so. Low self-esteem makes us too vulnerable to bring others together with us. But self-esteem says that if people can see who we are, it's worth a look. While many people with a poor self-image can ferociously pursue relationships, they often lack true intimacy.

2. Actively seek the job you love. There are reasons why many people stay in jobs they hate. Many people say they feel trapped, and, for some, the options are limited by the circumstances. But for all the people stuck in a job they don't like, there are a dozen

others who stay in unsatisfactory jobs out of sheer inertia. Self-esteem inspires us to reach for the stars, not because we are as tall as or better than others, but because we know it is perfectly natural to want to be satisfied and productive at work.

3. Valuing honesty in oneself and others. People with low self-esteem can use dishonesty to protect themselves or others from certain real or imagined consequences of telling the truth. Individuals with high self-esteem know that they can override the consequences of telling the truth, if necessary. Self-esteem and dishonesty and are like oil and water. Being a fundamentally honest person makes no effort when you are honest, which is good self-esteem.

4. Accepting the quality of your life. People with high self-esteem tend to have something called a "place of internal control." It means they believe in their ability to influence the character and course of their lives. The inverse of an internal locus of control is an external locus of control, which declares that life is like a lottery; you get sick, pull or take a bus due to the circumstances, and absolutely nothing you can do about it. But getting the flu shot, changing your work habits at the first sign that your boss is upset, and looking back and forth before crossing the street are some of the things you can do if you want to be fully responsible for your life.

5. Taking care of your physical health. Adequate concern for your physical health is a sign of self-esteem, as this concern is only possible if you appreciate yourself.

To neglect, mistreat or mistreat the body is to refuse responsibility for the quality of life. Please bear in mind that you can't always tell who cares about their health simply by looking at them; some people who look healthy are careless to themselves. Many people who do not meet society's standards for a "healthy" appearance are diligent in personal care.

6. Liking kids. It is complex and controversial. Some people who dislike children may be partial to adult logic, calm, or a lack of germs.

But for many people it's because being with children puts them in touch with parts of themselves that feel weak, small, or vulnerable. These people were often treated without sufficient empathy when they were children. They learned that children don't matter or that they are irritating, stupid, etc. You cannot have healthy self-esteem if you do not appreciate and embrace all parts of yourself, including the injured child inside.

7. Avoiding self-destructive behaviors. There are many ways to self-destruct. Addictions, bad financial decisions, reckless driving, and dangerous relationships are just a few examples. People who love them avoid situations and invent problems because inviting them does not make sense for those who appreciate and appreciate their quality of life.

Low self-esteem, on the other hand, says, "Who cares? I don't care. I'm not worth saving from trouble" or "I like problems; at least it's familiar." Self-destructive impulses can only exist when there is not enough self-esteem. Who would want to destroy someone they care about?

8. Taking calculated risks. Self-esteem is about success because success is a natural state for those who positively view themselves and others. To succeed, you sometimes have to take risks that can be scary. People with good self-esteem can move forward, even on an uncertain path, when the alternative is stagnation. Their integrity forces them to aim for personal goals, even when the result is not guaranteed. They know that the greatest regrets in life are not the things we tried that didn't work, but the things we never tried.

9. Building up other people. Self-esteem is a gift for us and others. We must not expend precious energy to defend ourselves against the insults imagined by our ability or to diminish others to make us feel better about ourselves. When we feel satisfied with who we are, we want others to be happy too. Validating other people is easy when we think our thoughts, feelings, and opinions matter. The great novelty of these good self-esteem indicators is that the signs and self-esteem are strengthened: if you act consistently as if you had high self-esteem, your self-esteem will increase. But don't take the word for it; try it yourself and see.

Is it Possible to Develop Our Self-Esteem Right Now?

If our self-esteem remains low, it will hinder our recovery, so, we have to strengthen it. What is wonderful is that it can be built at any time of life, regardless of age, level of education, and social position. Building self-esteem is certainly a slow process that requires a lot of patience and persistence. But it's worth it. It is important to remember that strong self-esteem evolves when you see yourself as a strong, precious, and helpful person, and it does not depend on how others see you. You are your greatest asset, and you can start improving your self-esteem today. What to do?

- Believe in yourself
- Leaving the past hurts and forgiving others
- Accepting and loving yourself unconditionally
- Plan and establish achievable goals in life
- Visualize yourself achieving and succeeding in life
- Internalize positive affirmations that help you believe in yourself

Some Suggestions to Strengthen Self-Esteem

Your self-esteem will affect all areas of your life. Your work, your relationships, and even your physical and mental health are a reflection of your self-esteem. But what exactly helps shape your vision of yourself and your skills? The truth about this is that your level of self-esteem may have increased or decreased depending on how you have been treated by people in the past and the assessments you have made about your life and choices.

The good news is that you have good control when you increase your level of self-esteem. You can make simple, concrete changes to test your mind and body. One of these changes is to take steps to reduce negative thinking and create positive and encouraging thoughts about who you are and who you can be.

Replace Negative Thinking with Positive Thinking

You can send negative messages about yourself. Many people do this. These are the messages you learned when you were young. You have learned from many different sources, including other children, their teachers, their families, caregivers, even the media, and the stigma and stigma in our society.

Here are some examples of common negative messages that people repeat to themselves: "I'm an idiot," "I'm a loser," "I never do anything well," "No one will ever love me," I'm a klutz. "Most people believe these messages, whether real or unreal. They come immediately under the right circumstances; for example, if you get the wrong answer, you think, "I'm so stupid. "They can include words as they should. Messages tend to imagine the worst of all things, especially you, and are difficult to turn off or not to learn.

You can think about these thoughts or transmit these negative messages to yourself so often that you barely notice them. Pay attention to them. Take a small notebook with you during your daily routine for several days and write down negative thoughts about yourself each time you notice them. Some people say they perceive more negative thoughts when tired, sick, or under a lot of stress. When you become aware of your negative thoughts, you can perceive them more and more.

Take an Inventory

If you are unsure of your self-esteem level, an inventory of your personal qualities may be useful. If you find more weaknesses than strengths, this can be a sign that you tend to be very hard on yourself. Think about the talents, skills, and passions that you have not listed or that you may not have discovered yet. Don't assume you know everything about yourself and what you can do.

Recognize Successes

Often people with low self-esteem dismiss their success as chance or luck. Or they could focus on not being perfect, rather than pointing out the road they have traveled. They say "thank you" when people congratulate them, rather than dismissing their praise. It does not mean that people with high self-esteem are arrogant or selfish; they trust their skills and recognize success when it happens.

Stop Comparing Yourself

Other people cannot be the norm when it comes to their self-esteem. It is because you will always find someone who looks better than you or more capable than you in any area of life. Social media is certainly not helpful, as researchers have found that people who control social media very often are more likely to suffer from low self-esteem. Remember that people usually only share the best parts of their lives online. Your life should be the criteria, not the lives of others, because what is best cannot belong to someone else and vice versa. Remember that every time you improve or stop making a mistake, you progress.

Chapter 12
Strategies for Developing Self-Esteem

Growing your self-esteem simply means starting to love yourself more. As you increase your self-love, it will become easier to strive for and reach your goals. You'll find that you are prepared to do the things it takes to lead a healthier, better life and be a better you. We will go over strategies that can be used to help grow your self-esteem.

Understand Your Life Story

From the moment you were born, the world around you started shaping your experience. The people in your early childhood, the experiences you had, and the way you developed all created the individual you are today. People often struggle with their life stories. They may look at their past with sadness or upset, particularly if they have had a hard life.

As you learn to love yourself, you come to appreciate what shaped you into the person you are today. It does not mean you have to love the hardships you faced. However, it can be useful to put them into perspective. People who experienced abuse at a young age may appreciate that they are stronger in relationships now and stand up for themselves. Someone who a bad dog bite might fight to understand why they are afraid of dogs.

Putting together your life story is like a puzzle. Every experience you had created memory in the subconscious, even if you cannot consciously remember it. As you look at your past, these pieces will eventually fall into place. As you understand who you are and why you are that way, you can appreciate yourself a lot more.

Treat Yourself

One of the reasons people with low self-esteem struggle in relationships is that they wait for their partner to make them feel special; while it is nice to have someone to give you recognition, it is essential for you to feel special. Stop waiting around for someone else to treat you. Set aside at least one day each week where you do something special for yourself. You might leave for work 15 minutes early so you can treat yourself to a gourmet coffee on the way to work or run yourself a bubble bath with candles and essential oils after a long day. Buy yourself the shirt or the belt that you have been looking at for months. Self-love is all about knowing you are unique. You do deserve to be treated—you just have to make it happen.

Express Your Insecurities

Unfortunately, it has also made keeping relationships more difficult. Remember the last time you went out with someone, and they were on their phone the entire time. Didn't you feel neglected? Something to remember in this situation is that the other person may not realize that their phone habits are upsetting you.

Additionally, many people see their cell phones as an addiction. They are always checking it because it has become second nature to them. Rather than becoming angry at the person, you are out with, it is essential to express how you feel. Care enough for yourself that you speak up and tell the person they are upsetting you. For most people, this will be enough for them to put down the phone and give you the attention you are asking for.

Your Self-Worth is Not Measured by Performance

Many people look at life as a competition, and when they are edged out by someone better, it can be detrimental to self-esteem. It is incredibly easy to link the things you do to the worth that you experience as a person. The reality is that you cannot use the things you have accomplished to measure your self-worth. Every person is on their unique journey. They succeed at different rates. It may be that the person who excelled has had more practice or that they prepared more. The thing more important than performance is a willingness to try. Every time that you try something new, you are stepping outside of your comfort zone.

Make a Difference

One of the reasons that some people feel they lack in life is because they are. When you live wholly for yourself, it can be hard to determine your self-worth outside of the company you work at or at home. One way to overcome a lack of purpose is to do something meaningful. Take a garbage bag to the woods or the beach and pick up trash. When you do things like this for others, it helps you make a difference in the way you feel about your self-worth as a person.

If you find your schedule a little busy for these charity activities, simply try kindness. When you are kind to the people around you, it makes a significant difference in your feelings about yourself. Empathy is also a decisive action that can set a chain of events in motion. These events can cause those around you to be kind to you as well. As you see that you are deserving of other people's kindness, you also realize that you are worthy of your own.

Stop Expecting Perfection

The idea of perfection is both unrealistic and harmful to your self-esteem. People get upset when they are not perfect because they live with the assumption that some others are. They always look great, meet all their deadlines, and never argue with coworkers. Remember that many people do not celebrate their mistakes. They are not at the office gossiping about how they procrastinated all weekend and had to stay up all night working on their project. Instead, they keep things calm and confident. They act as if they got the project done Friday night and spent the rest of the week-end relaxing.

Even when things seem perfect, they rarely are. Everyone makes mistakes—they just do not always make them public. People do not like to be seen as flawed, even though faulty behavior is entirely human. Though it can be hard to be seen as imperfect in social situations, stop expecting yourself to be unflawed. Always remember that you are only human as are the people around you. Even though you do not see their mistakes, they do exist.

Be Grateful

It is simple to be lost in negative emotions when you do not appreciate your life. By taking the time daily to appreciate what is going right in your life, you show self-love. You are also giving yourself time to realize that not everything about your life is negative. There are many positive experiences and elements of your life to be grateful for. Even something as simple as waking up in the morning or knowing that you have a warm house and food to come back to after work is something to be grateful for.

Make being grateful for a habit. Try to find at least 3-5 positive things each day that you can be grateful for. Keep in mind that you will notice these things more when you are mindful as you go through life. You cannot appreciate the blooming flowers that signify the start of spring if you are planning out your day on your way to work.

See Criticism as an Opportunity to Grow

People with low self-esteem or confidence may look too closely at criticism. They may see it as another thing they need to improve on, and it can bring down someone who is already feeling defeated. Instead of looking at criticism as a negative, look at it as an opportunity to grow. Do not forget that not a single person in the world is perfect. It is a person's quirks and imperfections that make them unique. Additionally, negative feedback is critical for realizing what changes you want to make. If you do not know what is wrong, it is impossible to make positive changes.

When a boss, coworker, relative, or acquaintance is continually speaking negatively about you, helping you improve is not necessarily their priority. Their constant criticism is best ignored, as it comes from a dangerous place.

Take Care of Yourself

If you love someone, would you feed them unhealthy food, make them stay up late hours of the night, and encourage them to sit on the couch instead of being active? No, you wouldn't. A significant part of developing your self-esteem is learning to take care of yourself. You cannot rely on other people to manage your life and be sure you are doing the right thing. Lack the self-esteem to take care of themselves is one of the reasons why people become obese. They continue with unhealthy habits because they do not want to change or do not believe that they are entitled to a higher quality of life. Taking care of yourself also applies to a mental aspect. It is important to enjoy the hard work you have done and relax. Love yourself enough that you slow down sometimes. If you push yourself too hard, your mind will eventually break.

The problem with failing to take care of yourself properly is that it is a slippery downward slope to less self-esteem. When you do not eat properly and exercise, it can cause health issues or obesity. These, in turn, can lead to lower self-esteem. Likewise, failing to get enough sleep affects your emotional regulation and cognitive abilities. It can also decrease self-esteem, as you may feel you cannot control your mind or incapable of doing the tasks you need to. Finally, when you do not take enough breaks from work, you may be critical about yourself when you cannot think clearly.

Instead of allowing these poor habits to impact your self-esteem negatively, treat yourself with love. Enrich your body with the right foods and try to avoid those things that poison it. Have enough responsibility and love for yourself to go to sleep on time, so you can wake up the next day and have the best possible chance of acting confident and reaching toward your goals. Finally, give yourself enough time to slow down and enjoy your life. Knowing that you deserve these treats can help you realize that you deserve the self-love that you neglect to give yourself sometimes.

Make the Toughest Thing on Your To-Do List Come First

Many tasks seem intimidating when you look at the whole picture. For example, someone who works during the week might spend Saturdays doing stuff around the house. If their to-do list is filled with chores like clean the gutters, scrub the bathtub, take out the trash and sweep the floors, it can be easy to keep putting off what they need to do. However, when the sun goes down, and they still have not done the most challenging thing on their list, the day seems as if it has been wasted.

Instead of putting off those tasks you do not want to do until last, get them out of the way first. The person above might tackle cleaning the gutters first. Additionally, by cleaning the gutters first, the most challenging job is out of the way, and everything else seems almost effortless by comparison.

Chapter 13
Positive Thinking

The Power of Positive Thinking

N negative thinking has a purpose. When humankind was still in its early days, there was no separation between humans and the world around them. There were no cities—they lived entirely in the wild. It meant they had to deal with the world's natural dangers, from predatory animals like tigers and bites from poisonous snakes. There was also the danger of other societies and the natural obstacles of the earth. It meant that even something like walking to the river had its risks.

This danger that existed in early society may be why strong, negative emotions like fear cause the brain and body to hyperdrive. At this moment, your mind stops and focuses on nothing but the wolf. An area of the amygdala sends messages through your brain and the rest of your body that there is danger. It triggers the fight-or-flight response, which lets you focus on survival. Perception intensifies as you analyze the situation again, and there is a boost to your reflexes and speed. Your blood pumps through your muscles, your breath rate increases to boost the amount of air moving through your lungs, and you are ready to run or fight off the wolf in front of you.

Of course, worrying that the worst-case scenario will come true (the wolf eating you) triggers this incredible survival response. In this scenario, it is remarkable that the mind tries its best to survive. However, this reaction to intense emotions and the fear of the worst happening is not necessarily practical in day-to-day life. When you are always thinking negatively and fearing the worst, those negative things will happen. As you create the reality of your life, choosing how to spend your time and focusing on your effort can make the reality of your positive or negative sense of well-being.

How Negative Thinking Holds You Back

When you focus on the intense, negative emotions, you are experiencing, your narrowed focus limits what you can think during that time. It becomes difficult to use rational thought to overcome your negative thinking. It is the reason why people have phobias and anxiety—their brains are extra-sensitive to stimuli around them. It triggers the fight-or-flight response even when there isn't any immediate danger. Likewise, negative thinking holds you back because it narrows your focus. It puts your thoughts in the habit of looking for the negatives. It means you do not see the opportunities or the positive elements of a situation.

Negative thinking also holds you back because it leaves you ill-adapted to stressful situations. Rather than looking for ways to overcome obstacles, you end up making problems bigger. People who do not try to overcome their problems and just accept them also get stuck in the same cycles. They cannot rise above or achieve success in life because they are stuck in the loop of their negative thoughts.

Finally, negative thinking causes you to discourage yourself. Rather than building yourself up and using self-talk in a way that encourages you to strive for your goals, it leaves you feeling defeated and incapable. After all, why should someone step out of their comfort zone if they "know" they will fail? By continuing to think negatively, people hold themselves back.

One study that explored the power of positive thinking was carried out at the University of North Carolina by psychology researcher, Barbara Frederickson. The experiment involved film clips and five different groups of people. Group 1 and 2 saw clips associated with positive emotions, with Group 1 seeing images that stimulated joy, and Group 2 saw pictures that produced contentment. Group 3 saw neutral pictures and was used as a control for the experiment. Groups 4 and 5 saw negative images, with Group 4 seeing images that stimulated fear, and Group 5 saw pictures that provoked anger.

Following the video, each participant was given a piece of paper with twenty blank lines and the instructions to imagine themselves in a situation that created the same feelings as the video they had watched. Then, they were to write down what they would do in this scenario. The results showed people who experienced anger and fear had the least responses, while those who experienced contentment and joy wrote the most responses. The neutral group generally fell in the middle of the average. It speaks to how positive emotions cause you to see more possibilities, leaving you open to the options all around you.

What is Positive Thinking?

Although the "positive" is meant to mean upbeat and happy, many people are confused about positive thinking. Does it mean that you are happy most of the time? Does it mean that you blissfully ignore problems to avoid stress? Not necessarily. Positive thinking is a mental state where you expect the best. You wish you to meet your goals, succeed in your dating life, and generally experience a good life. It does not indicate that you will never deal with negativity—it is natural for people to experience things like job loss, the death of a loved one, and break-ups. Life is not perfect, and it does throw curveballs.

When this happens, however, positive thinking is knowing that you are strong enough to overcome. You believe that you are tough enough to grieve and continue living or pick yourself up and find a new job. It indicates that when issues arise, you are proactive about solving them. You use constructive and critical thinking to come up with solutions.

Additionally, by thinking positively, you do not assume the worst of people. You are more likely to look for concrete evidence before making assumptions. Finally, a positive mindset is motivated and generally happy. You are excited about the future because you know it will offer you new opportunities and bring you closer to your goals.

How You Can Use Positive Thinking to Build Confidence and Self-Esteem

When you think positively, it stays with you for several minutes. However, research shows that when you use that positive attitude to develop resources and build skills, it increases your learning ability. Take the example of a child who is playing outside. He may be running around a field or swinging on a vine (physical skills) while playing with friends (social skills). Additionally, his observation and exploration of the world around him engage his creative talents. As running around, exploring, and playing with friends are enjoyable, the positive emotions make it more likely that he will continue building their physical, social, and creative skills by playing outside.

Even once that child has gone off to college, his athletic skills might earn him a scholarship or a place playing professional sports, while his social skills may give him the option to work closely with a team of people or run a business. Even though the skills remain, the person might not feel those initial positive feelings that helped them learn the craft. By contrast, negative emotions have the opposite effect. When you are experiencing negative emotions like those, you would feel when in danger, your mind is only focused on what is happening at that immediate time. It means you cannot focus on building skills that will benefit you in the future.

Strategies for Increasing Positive Thinking

Frederickson's research developed the "broaden and build" theory. It simply states that by thinking positively, you broaden your ability to see more possibilities around you. Once your perspective is enlarged, you can develop skills that add value to your life.

Here are a few ways to increase positive thought:

Do something you love. Even doing something like painting or playing the guitar has benefits (expressing yourself abstractly and helping with stress management). As an added benefit, when you love something, you become passionate about it. It is easy to be optimistic about an activity you enjoy.

Write. The Journal of Research in Personality published a study that involved 90 students separated into two groups. Group 1 wrote about a positive experience for three days in a row, while the second group was assigned a control topic. After just three days of this practice, the students in Group 1 had improved mood levels, fewer illnesses, and few visits to the health center. When you write positively, even a few days in a row, it would seem to impact your overall level of health and happiness profoundly.

Meditate daily. Not only does meditation help increase your self-awareness, but it also helps increase positivity. Its effects are long term, according to a more recent study carried out by Frederickson and fellow researchers. Two months after the end of the course, those meditated people displayed a decrease in illnesses, a sense of purpose in life, mindfulness, and better social support.

Make time for play. Slaving away at work day after day means nothing if you cannot enjoy life. After all, why do you strive for a new car if you do not have the time to drive it? Why buy a lovely house if you are never home to enjoy it? It is essential to enjoy yourself intentionally. Don't save it for the last minute—write it in your schedule and make time for it. When you live more positively, you'll find you are more productive and goal-minded when working.

Remember that everything changes. Life is about transformation. Every time you acquire a new skill or overcome an obstacle, you are one step closer to your total transformation. It is also an excellent way to look at negative situations that you cannot control. Even though someone may be sad after a parent passes away, their negative feelings will eventually die, and they will learn to live without their parent's physical presence in the world.

By developing more incredible willpower, getting in the habit of setting goals, and creating more positive thought patterns, you can set yourself up for success in life. As you continue to read, you'll gain more insight into how these strategies can be applied to grow your confidence and self-esteem.

Your "Why"

When you recognize what you want to accomplish, characterize your "why". Consider what it will intend to you when you achieve this unequivocal result. Imagine yourself having finished it. Directly beneath your goal, record whatever achieving this particular goal intended for you. It is your self-inspirational power for making a move.

Your Massive Plan of Action

Alright, you have what you might want to be characterized and you know why you want it. Presently ask yourself, "What are the moves I should make to accomplish my result?" Write them out.

Goal setting and planning encourage you to see what you have to do. The way to getting results is by making a move. Concentrate on what you have recorded and pick what you can do right away. Creating a predictable movement is a crucial fixing strategy that gets results. At the point when you get moving, energy becomes an integral factor. You will achieve your particular result and make the most of your "why".

Do this uncomplicated goal setting and planning framework vigorously for each result you have recorded. Set aside a period consistently to utilize this procedure and make a move each day. Over the long haul, you will be astounded at how a lot of your life winds up better.

Chapter 14
Lack of Motivation

How to Beat a Lack of Motivation

When you lose your motivation, you often lack the reason you want to accomplish something. There are numerous reasons why you feel this way. Some reasons could include that you're not interested in the goal, you do not feel that the reward is enough, or perhaps you just don't see the point. To increase your motivation again, you need to change your thought process and look inside yourself for motivation. Otherwise, there's no point.

Say you are feeling overwhelmed. If the goal is too overwhelming, you may feel dread and procrastinate or simply not see yourself as successful. How can you change this? Break the goal into smaller steps to feel less overwhelmed. Visualize yourself completing the goal and being successful. When you see yourself finishing something, the success you feel just by visualizing it will often be enough to motivate you.

A Lack of Self-Confidence

Perhaps you have stopped believing in yourself. If this has happened, you will probably experience negative or destructive self-talk. In effect, you will experience doubts about your success.

How can you change this? Start by looking at past successes. Think about other ways that you have achieved your goals and spend some time looking back on them. You also need to limit your negative beliefs about yourself and use affirmations or positive statements.

Lack of Time or Energy

When you feel like you lack motivation, consider that you could just be exhausted. Is there too much going on in your life, are you just worn out, or do you have no room in your life to pursue your goals? If you feel like this is you, here are some tips to get your motivation back.

<u>No is an acceptable answer</u> so start by saying no. It is more important than you may realize, and if we say yes to everything, we get burnt out. Consider starting a <u>journal</u> or perhaps learning <u>meditation</u>. Both of these will allow you to free up mental as well as physical energy. Once you free up space, the motivation to pursue your goals should return.

Fear is a reality and often discounted when infecting our lives. When you lack motivation because of fear, you may not even realize that fear is holding you back. Perhaps you are afraid that you will embarrass yourself, or you are afraid to fail. Another reason could be that the unknown makes you fearful, or perhaps the idea of being successful makes you afraid.

When you look at your life, are you experiencing the following symptoms: procrastination, anxiety, resistance, or excessive worrying? If you are, you need first to pinpoint what you are afraid of; after you do that, you need to determine why you are afraid.

Your Health is Suffering

Perhaps you are unable to feel the motivation to pursue your goals because you are ill, or you have been leading an unhealthy lifestyle that is finally starting to catch up to you. If you feel sluggish, tired, or have chronic pain, you could be experiencing these because of your lifestyle. If you have brain fog, or the inability to focus, you could have lost your motivation due to your lifestyle. This one is a somewhat simple fix: consider adopting a healthier way of living. Look to change your diet, your exercise routine, or seek medical care.

The Goals that You Have Set are Too Small or Too Big

If you set goals that are too small, it will not inspire you to complete them; besides, creating goals that are too high or too big will make you feel like you do not have the confidence to accomplish them. To avoid this, make your goals reachable. Set the goals that allow you to achieve success, but make them just far enough to reach that you grow in the process. Prepare yourself up for success for you to feel good about yourself.

Are you are impatient? One of the final reasons that you could be lacking the motivation to finish your goals is because you simply think that you should have reached them by now. Impatience will cause you to quit often before you even start. You'll quit because you feel like it's taken too long to reach your goals. To combat this, you need to take pleasure in the journey and understand that the progress you are making will take time. As your accomplishing the small steps, consider rewarding yourself for your progress. When you acknowledge the progress you've made, you slow down and see that you are accomplishing something.

Tips for Succeeding

When you are setting your goals, you need to find out why you want to achieve them. What is the force behind your motivation? As you are considering the force behind your motivation, make sure that the reasons for pursuing a goal are strong enough. Also, make sure that the proper motivation is there. When you set small, weak goals, you are not giving yourself a chance to feel motivated by them. Consider what you will gain when you complete your goals and make sure that is enough to motivate you.

See your success using visualization techniques, and use them when you can. Visualize yourself being successful and experience the emotions that come with that success. Also, visualize yourself feeling failure. Allow yourself to feel all the emotions that come along with failing. It is important because it can motivate you to continue.

It's a good idea to ensure that the environment you are in is supportive. When you do this, your confidence will increase. The more rooting people, the better you will feel as you pursue your goals. It is important to surround yourself with people who support the work you are trying to do.

Perspective matters so consider changing your perspective on life. Do you have a positive perspective or a negative one? If you tend to look at life and see the positive things, motivation may not be an issue for you. However, if you look at life and tend to focus on the negative, try making a habit of looking for the good things life offers. They are there, and you have to look for them. Sometimes, they are small things such as a baby laughing or getting inside before it rains. Other times, they are big, and you will notice them. You were focusing on the positive rather than the negative will help you change your outlook on life.

Seek help and find motivation through others, such as a life coach, friends, or mentors. When you see someone successful and admire them, consider finding out their tips and secrets. More often than not, people will be happy to help you out. One day, when you get the chance, make sure that you help someone as well.

Go big, start small. Get yourself going and make sure that your dreams are big but you are starting small. No matter what it takes, you are getting started. As you go along the journey, take breaks and rest so as not to lose your momentum. Your goals are achievable, and you deserve to make them a reality.

Our emotions can either control us or help us. If we allow them to control us, we are harming ourselves and our relationships. When we allow our emotions to help us, we can learn to harness the power behind them. We feel the emotions can keep us from harm, spur on change, and manipulate our situations. By learning to harness the power behind them, we are using every resource available to us.

When we look at the emotions that run through our bodies, they can be intimidating and complex. But when we know how to harness the power, we can gain the success that we didn't know was possible.

Defining Self-Defeating Thoughts

When people happen to be depressed or anxious, or low on self-esteem, they react to everything present around them. Under this condition, they develop the habit of overthinking almost everything present near them, be it something that concerns them or not. This habit of overthinking leads them to affirm the negative thoughts that shroud their rationality.

Once a negative thought challenges an individual who is already having a tough time trying to fight depression or anxiety, he (or she) can do nothing besides bowing down to them. Such individuals bow down to these thoughts and reaffirm whatever negative opinions they have about themselves. They build upon the negative beliefs and contribute to their fears and support an already depleted self-esteem.

This distorted thinking has been distributed into numerous types by prominent psychologists. Psychologists call this style of thinking distorted thinking because you distort reality to look at things the way your mind wants you to. You're painting a gloomy picture of the things around you, and the negativity around you so deludes you that you are not trying to counter the negative thoughts through the pervasive power of positive thoughts.

Realize Negative Events

Behind every negative thought you come across, there has to be an adverse event instigating that pattern. Just like we have seen so many times above, the negative thoughts you encounter are part of a special type of thinking pattern that you have developed over time. You look for evidence to prove this thinking pattern and don't look for evidence other than that.

Now, when it comes to identifying the self-defeating thoughts you encounter, you need first to identify the events that caused such a reaction. If we go by the principles of cause and effect, every response in this world is caused by a past action. The reaction that you are undergoing is an event you have encountered.

What made you feel that you aren't good for this world and are unlovable? What made you host this particular perception? What was that specific feeling that got you thinking in this manner? Was it a message from an ex-friend? Was it something nice that someone did to you? Or was it because you started comparing yourself to others?

You must find out what makes you go deep into the world of wonderland and distorted thinking. The things influencing your negative thoughts need to be clarified, and you need to view them without any obstructions. Only when you identify what exactly is pushing you through the negativity can you help spot where the problems lie?

For instance, most people go into distorted thinking when they consider themselves guilty. Your team at work wasn't able to achieve its objectives. You had a wrong thought about a relationship that just ended or had a bad time comparing your family to others. You then go for the easy way out and start thinking negatively. You have been conditioned to think negatively, which is why no other option spring into your mind.

Conclusion and Remarks

Asking yourself the "what can I do question" in various situations and areas of your life will allow you to challenge your mind to develop solutions and plans that bring forth the actualization of aims, goals, and dreams. For instance, if you want a great relationship, "what can you do" to ensure that your aim becomes your daily life?

This question makes you more purposeful about your pursuit, and when you are purposeful, you are more assured and confident. You are the only person capable of deciding what you want, what you have to do to achieve it, and what it means to you. Take responsibility for yourself and your life by taking responsibility for your daily time and life.

The more responsible you are with your time, resources, attention, intention, and effort, the likelier you will be more successful, confident, and purposeful. You are also likely to be happier with yourself and where you are, which is on the path to daily personal development in major areas of your life.

To achieve your aims and aspirations, of which you probably have many, you have to be responsible for how you use your time and resources. Instead of multitasking or pursuing many goals simultaneously, which is likely to lead to overwhelm, low motivation and low self-confidence, pursue one goal at a time, solve one problem at a time every single day.

By narrowing your intention and attention, i.e., what you want and what you have to do to achieve it - which requires time - you become surer of the effort you must take to achieve your primary aim. This clarity allows you to be purposeful with your daily habits, time, effort, and overall wellbeing as you pursue your goals, aim, dreams, and aspirations.

Many of us know the changes we need to address to make our lives better but we often fail to do so and instead opt to maintain the status quo. To become more purposeful and therefore more confident and self-assured, adopt a new mentality, a mentality that allows you to stop postponing yourself, your goals and aspirations, while you neglect the very things your psyche truly craves.

Whenever you set an intention, decide to do or improve something, take immediate action. Use the now mentality so you can create the momentum you need to achieve success in the key pillars of your life.

Becoming purposeful becomes possible when you adopt what you want to achieve as an integral part of your daily life. Adopting the habit of purposeful practice allows you to become intentional with your daily pursuits and recognize the results of these pursuits on your overall wellbeing, peace of mind, success, and confidence. Whether you are working on the spiritual, physical, or mental aspect of your life, make its practice an integral component of your daily life. Consistent practice is the difference between self-actualization and a life floundering in discontentment and unfulfilled potential.

Your vision is a representation of what you would like to achieve within specific areas of your life. When you have a clear vision of the achievements you would like to attain under your belt or the kind of person you would like to be one, five, or ten years from now, it gives you the clarity needed to be purposeful with using all your resources including intention, attention, time, energy and effort.

Create a vision board, or a sort of master timeline, to show what you intend to achieve and the kind of person you want to become. At the start of each endeavor or aim, have an intention - the desired outcome. For instance, at the start of the day, set the intention to be more mindful and purposeful with your decisions and actions.

Attaching intentions to all your decision, aims, endeavors, and daily undertakings allows you to reconnect with the present moment, who you are or want to become, and determine whether the intention and attention given to the activity are congruent with your desires or aims. By choosing how you want to be, feel, or act, you become more purposeful, at peace and content, and more successful and confident in key areas of your life.

Having a grand purpose or vision for your life is great. Still, to achieve anything substantial and move forward with poise and confidence, you also need to think small and infuse simplicity into your grand scheme because only by doing so can you curtail the human tendency to overestimate what we can achieve within a given period.

Have a grand dream, yes, but break it down into simple steps that build up to that make it easier to achieve. When you are purposeful, you avoid feeling overwhelmed and instead become surer of your decisions and actions, knowing that their undertaking helps create the life you want to live.

Rest is a highly underrated part of our daily lives, and it is typically the first area to be impacted when we are feeling stressed or unwell. We begin to find ourselves sleeping less, feeling more restless when we sleep, or not feeling fully rested when we wake. Soon, we skip exercising because we are too tired. We begin to skip it entirely which becomes a habit. Before we know it, we also skip eating healthy meals because we feel too tired to prepare them. The spiral continues until we are in a rut, feeling that we are at our worst with poor exercise and diet habits, and an even worse sleeping pattern.

It is important that, unless mandatory, you refrain from using any chemical sleep aids. Supplements and medicines can inhibit the body's natural ability to sleep on your own without their support. Furthermore, they can prevent you from having a truly restful sleep by manufacturing one for you. In short, life changes when there is inattention to self-care and it comes from low self-esteem.

Possessing low self-esteem may result in people being discouraged, falling short of their ability, or tolerating abusive relationships and circumstances. It can also be a symptom of pathological narcissism in which individuals can act in a self-centered, selfish, and dishonest manner.

Including academic and professional achievement, in friendships and mental health, self-esteem affects life in so many ways. Nevertheless, self-esteem is not an immutable characteristic; both personal and professional achievements and failures will cause variations in one's sense of self-worth. Self-esteem has been shown to influence physical and mental well-being and health-related attitudes, and then long-term health and well-being-related habits in adulthood. Working on self-esteem is a handy tool for health professionals during their encounters with clients, staff, other healthcare team members, hospitals, and medical students. People with low self-esteem consider many flaws in themselves, whether real or not, and it must be addressed. They are too eager to please and win the affections of other people so as not to offend them. They are also jealous of others with the characteristics and possessions that they want to have. They have an aura of hate around them and no excuse to be irritable. They focus on the thoughts and compliments of other people to draw an image of their worth.

Low self-esteem sounds dreadful, doesn't it? It is a good thing that it can be improved. It is hard to change one's attitudes and behaviors but I have shown that it can happen and when it does, it will change your life. Get on board with other survivors of low self-esteem and enjoy a richer and more rewarding life.

www.ingramcontent.com/pod-product-compliance
Lightning Source LLC
Chambersburg PA
CBHW060940050726

47592CB00003B/1044